8 Days

&

Virtue

Andrew McNabb

DIVINE PROVIDENCE PRESS

Milwaukee, Wisconsin

Copyright © 2014 by Andrew McNabb and
Divine Providence Press
www.divineprovidencepress.com
Divine Providence Press is an imprint of
Wiseblood Books
www.wisebloodbooks.com

Printed in the United States of America
Set in Arabic Typesetting

Library of Congress Cataloging-in-Publication Data
McNabb, Andrew, 1968-
8 Days & Virtue/ Andrew McNabb;
1. McNabb, Andrew, 1968-
2. Spiritual Memoir
3. Paean

ISBN-13: 978-0692217221
ISBN-10: 0692217223

8 Days

&

Virtue

Andrew McNabb

CONTENTS

8 DAYS

VIRTUE

Prologue

I have lived an American life not unlike many others. I was raised in the suburbs by loving parents. I was a good, but not exceptional, student. I played sports and had friends and did the sometimes-smart, but oftentimes-foolish things that teenagers do.

I went to college. I got a job. I got a better job. I changed careers. I fell in love. I got married. My wife and I had children. We are raising them the best we can, and not unlike the way we were raised. Life is good.

But while my life has not been unlike many others, there is no such thing as an unexceptional existence. Though our broad strokes may be recognizable, we do not live in broad strokes but in the saturating intensity of each moment, no matter how seemingly mundane. These moments are so singular to each of us, and thus we are all so eminently exceptional.

Throughout all these many days and weeks and years that I have lived, throughout the struggle and the growth, from the forgotten to the remembered, from the self-destruction to the healing, from the restlessness and longing inherent in our exile from Him, to the feeling, at times, of joy or even simple well-being, I have come to recognize every bit the import that has been assigned to each of our lives—to yours and mine both—and it is clear that no two paths to Him, or away from Him, are the same. And so in this we are all extraordinary, exceptional; this is the very heart of our human condition. We are all extraordinary, exceptional, in that we even exist at all.

Still, as a sign of the infinitude of His love for us, in addition to the great gift of life itself, we can be given things that are truly remarkable, perhaps even unspeakably good. In my life that has not been unlike many others, I have, in fact, received such a gift, one that I am by no means worthy of, and one which, in the simple context of this book before you, and in the simple context of my life as I am living it, I am now compelled to share.

In my life of recognizable broad strokes, of familiar small moments, something quite unusual and remarkable did happen to me: on the morning of November 2nd, 2011, All Souls Day, God visited me.

At the very moment that I typed the word that would complete the book I was writing about virtue, the Holy Spirit entered my body—my living soul—without warning and with such merciful fury that I was knocked to the ground in fits of ecstasy, my very foundation literally, figuratively toppled. His coming marked the beginning of an eight-day period of spiritual elevation, in which I experienced similar acts of direct union with God the Father and with Jesus Christ, His Son. While my experiences were bewilderingly good and overtly divine, I also suffered great physical and spiritual and emotional withdrawal (indeed, I wanted what I was experiencing to stop). But perhaps most disturbingly, in addition to all the good, I was also given an awareness of the real presence of evil, and even interaction with it.

Needless to say, my life has been forever changed. Though a good and faithful Catholic, this grace was, obviously, never anticipated. As I write this, I find myself in the midst of spiritual conversion, one brought about through prayer, daily Mass, a lay Dominican vocation, and with the fruits accorded me in my desire (however imperfect in practice) to submit to God's plan for me. Part of this plan, I know now, is to let others know about my experiences.

In this regard, I must say that there are really no words to describe the incomparable joy, the incalculable love, the ineffable goodness, the indescribable majesty, the overwhelming—indeed, at times quite frightening—power of His triune presence. Please forgive, then, the shortcomings of my utterly human effort.

Still, though my words may fail to capture what I experienced, what is most important is that it happened—and not that it happened to me, but that it happened *at all*. In a world that is increasingly turning away from Him and His Truth, in a society that is progressively marginalizing religion's role in our lives, and in a culture that is ever more skeptical of, even indignant towards, the concept of the Divine, I can say, joyfully, "It's all true!"

As a recipient of the greatest gift a human can receive, I no longer have to rely exclusively on faith. I have experienced Truth in a way so few people do. I have experienced some small part of Him. *Me*, this ordinary man. Me, this pathetic, sinful, privileged man who had done nothing, nothing at all on my own to warrant this grace. I am not even the best person in my own home. Why He chose me I do not know except to say that He often chooses the weak and unexceptional to do His work. I know full-well the implications of this admission, but if my revealing this personal truth in this troubled and confused age can influence even one soul toward Him, then woe to me if I conceal it.

Which leads, finally, to what is "It?" What is the "It" in "It's all true"? To be sure, I do not have all the answers, I can only draw reference to the context in which I experienced these graces. As I mentioned, my experiences were Trinitarian in nature and my worship in the context of a devout Catholic faith. The one thing I can say with all certainty is that we need Him. We need Him, and the farther we recede from Him, the farther we recede from who and what we really are. We have been created in His image, and He is perfection, the very definition of beauty. And so we are to be beautiful, and beautiful according to the way in which He wants us to be beautiful. Our attempt to enact this in our lives—to, in St. Thomas Aquinas's words, "live rightly"—is, quite simply, to employ virtue: Faith, Hope, Love; Justice, Prudence, Temperance, and Fortitude.

While my experiences are inextricably woven into the book I wrote, *Virtue*, time and providence have allowed me an additional perspective, an understanding that *Virtue* is not the sole writing to be put forth. Accordingly, following immediately after this prologue, and preceding my treatise, *Virtue*, you will find a detailed account of what I experienced during those eight days, followed by an epilogue.

As for *Virtue* itself, I have moved beyond the trepidation I initially experienced in letting it go. In those early weeks and months when I was still struggling to understand what had happened to me, I had attached an enormous personal weight to the book. While *Virtue* was, no doubt, a catalyst for my experiences, it is by no means *the cause* of those experiences. What I have experienced was given to me by God, Himself, for reasons only He knows. As such, I make no claim as to *Virtue's* worth. That can only be determined by the individual. I can only say that what started off as a literary exercise from a career short-story writer turned into something quite different.

Sincerely, and in Him,

Andrew McNabb
Portland, Maine
May, 2013

8 Days:
A Spiritual Memoir

Day One

Wednesday, November 2, 2011

Day One began like most other weekdays during that time in my life. I don't recall exactly what time I arose, but five-thirty would be typical. My routine was to head downstairs from my third-floor bedroom to the first floor, where I would make coffee, say the morning prayers from the *Magnificat*, and then head quietly back upstairs to my office, which is just off my bedroom. In my office I would read *The New York Times* on-line, pay bills and take care of light correspondence, while working to free my mind in preparation for the day's writing.

I was still, at the time, settling into a new writing routine. My wife and I have four children, just four years apart oldest to youngest. It was important to us to raise our children ourselves until they were ready to go off to school. Given my profession I had the flexibility to do that, and given the financial realities of my job relative to my wife's, it made sense that I would be the one at home with them. I had been used to writing right up until my wife left for her sales job between eight-thirty and nine, but beginning that September my schedule had become a little freer, with my two younger children, twins, now spending their mornings in a city-run pre-k program. I was responsible for driving them out to their school on the outer edge of the city, while my wife would walk my older two to the elementary school across the street from our house. Since September I had been waiting to begin writing until after dropping off my twins, but on that morning, I decided to start early.

I was motivated, because I knew I was getting close to finishing the book I had been writing about Christian virtue. I had started the process sixteen months prior, a process which included, in a first for me, a good deal of research. When I sat down that early-morning, I intended to do what I frequently did, and that was to read my last few paragraphs from the previous day so that I could think about them in preparation for a full writing session after drop-off. But in reading, I was inclined to edit, and then write.

I was writing about love, the book's necessary ending. I typed, at times with my eyes closed, the early morning sun shining in on my face. The writing was flowing, so intensely, yet so freely. I felt the words bringing me close, closer. The words, so free. Word upon word, active, yet led, to that end, to that ending, to the last word, to the period that would end it all... and precisely then, at that very moment, the course of my life changed forever...

But before I go further I should stop and explain a little bit about my career as a writer and about the book I was writing. I have had a modest career. At the time, I had been writing full-time for thirteen years, with the entirety of my published work being short-stories.

Though classified by some as a "Catholic" writer, my stories had been published in a variety of venues, from prominent mainstream literary journals like *The Missouri Review*, *The Potomac Review*, *Many Mountains Moving* and others, to dedicated Christian literary journals, to fine arts quarterlies, to a variety of anthologies, including *Not Safe, But Good* (*Best Christian Short Stories, 2007*) (Thomas Nelson). I had one published book to my credit, a short-story collection entitled, *The Body of This* (1st Edition, 2009, Warren Machine Books. 2nd Edition, 2014, Wiseblood Books.) *The Body of This* was well-reviewed in both the secular and Catholic presses, and found a distinct audience among what might be termed "highly literate" Catholics. The book was well-received by this audience but was not without its detractors, with the majority opinion among the dissenters that the book was too "visceral" for a proper Catholic audience. Indeed the book addresses the various and not always comely aspects of our physical selves and the choices we make with our bodies. I can say here that my intent with these stories, and with everything I have ever written, was to praise the unsurpassed beauty and goodness of God and His creation. There can be no loftier goal for an artist, and one is bound to come up short, as I am sure I did. Nevertheless, I was, and am, proud of the book and my effort.

The publishing of *The Body of This* was clearly an important step in my career. Over the fourteen months following the release of the book I wrote more stories. By and large, these stories did not work. Emotionally and spiritually I had moved on from the dominant subject matter contained in the collection; subject matter that was rooted, largely, in the sins of my youth. The stories I was writing lacked freshness and originality, but I was reluctant to move beyond them, and beyond the genre. I had always written short. Even my short stories were short. As a writer with aspirations and an eye on the marketplace, I was attempting to carve out a niche: Catholic short-story writer. Flannery O'Connor was not my ideal in this regard, but the non-Catholic Lydia Davis. I recognized a like-minded spirit in the curt and evocative emotionalism of her stories, and I envisioned myself as a sort of devout Catholic version of her. Needless to say, that didn't really work out. It was tough moving on.

I have not been prolific when it comes to completed works. I have started many writing projects only to abandon them after a week, a month, a year. I came to writing relatively late, at age thirty, and seeing another good chunk of time disappear without credit was difficult. I wasn't getting any younger, and I wasn't particularly inspired. I had four young children, whom I adored and took good care of, but my responsibility in taking care of them was, at times, overwhelming. My wonderful wife went off to work each day to keep our entire operation afloat, and though she did it joyfully, as she does everything, she would rather have been at home with the kids. This was difficult for me, at times, and it was a further burden to not be helping financially as much as I wanted to. But if there was a true burden in my life at the time, it was I, myself. For as long as I have been writing, my very identity and self-worth have been intertwined with the craft. This association was so intense, in fact, that it had led me into a depression a number of years before; a depression that was still persistent through that time. The ultimate hope, the hope inherent in recognizing Christ risen, never wavered and never left me, but in terms of my own idea of success or failure in this life, I myself was in my own way.

I won't say that I ever hit rock bottom—in fact, I will say that I have never hit rock bottom, because something has always kept me afloat, and this something is not of me or from me, yet it kept me in the light, even on my darkest days. At some point in the early summer of 2010, after abandoning the follow-up collection to *The Body of This*, I had made up my mind (or was otherwise inspired) to simply let God lead me. This intent related to my life in general, of course, but very specifically to my writing.

I began to write an epistolary novel. In those early stages, virtue was emerging as the primary topic between my two conversants. The piece was fictional, but the more I wrote, the less so it was becoming. My knowledge of the intellectual and theological underpinnings of Christian virtue was not extensive, and I knew that if I were to proceed with any measure of success I would have to change that. My first step was to return to a book that had had a major influence on my life, St. Francis de Sales's *Introduction to the Devout Life*. St. Francis was born in Savoy in 1567. He is known for his deep faith, his gentle yet uncompromising handling of the religious divisions of the time, and his spiritual writings. In fact, he is the patron saint of writers. Back in 2000, when I had first taken up writing full-time, I began to seek his help and intercession. To do so properly I bought and read this most famous book of his.

Introduction to the Devout Life, written in 1609 (and completed in its final form in 1619,) is derived, interestingly enough, from a correspondence St. Francis de Sales was having with a devoted young woman, Madame Charmoisy, wife of the Duke of Savoy. Philothea ("Lover of God") as he refers to her in the text, was finding it difficult to live a life devoted to God given her courtly duties and way of life. To aid her, St. Francis provided an outlined guide detailing the practical employment of virtue, instructing and bringing her through the ascending stages of the rising spiritual journey. The final stage of the devout life leads, ultimately, to at least partial participation in Him. The form this participation takes will be, of course, different for different people, but what will remain the same is a unitive experience. It was only after my own physical experiences of God that I came to fully understand why this book is commonly referred to as a mystical text.

At a crossroads, and trying to figure out if what I was writing was fiction or non-fiction, and needing, either way, a deeper understanding of virtue, I left

Maine in August 2010 for a week in Santa Fe, New Mexico. I had received a scholarship to attend The Glen Workshops, a workshop and retreat run by the Christian Literary and Arts Organization, *IMAGE*. It was there that I began a deep and studious re-reading of St. Francis's *Introduction*. Over the course of the week I managed to write a summary of each of the one-hundred nineteen exercises and instructions that comprised the book. The experience was enlightening, inspiring, and affirming and I returned home to my family with great resolve.

I would indeed be writing about virtue, and most likely, I decided, in a non-fiction format. I spent the rest of 2010 reading and studying some of the many papal encyclicals, apostolic letters and theological tracts addressing Christian virtue. I also studied scripture, seeking to identify the many references, overt and implied, to virtue and its practice.

I derived particular benefit from the Bible, of course, but also from Pope Benedict XVI's encyclicals *Deus Caritas Est* (God is Love), *Spe Salvi* (In Hope We Are Saved), and other of his writings, from the *Catechism of the Catholic Church*, Josef Pieper's extensive writings on the topic, the portions of St. Thomas Aquinas's *Summa* devoted to virtue, and bits and pieces from many other sources.

But, perhaps more than any other document, or simply a teaching from any other document, it was the Universal Call to Holiness as espoused in *Lumen Gentium*, one of the principal documents of the Second Vatican Council, that became a seminal influence.

While some may contend that the intent of this call is simply to urge the faithful to "live well" in their faith, brought to its logical end this call to holiness can only mean, ultimately, the pursuit of *perfection*. A common misunderstanding insists that such a lofty goal can easily lead one into the sin of scrupulosity, or even despair in failure. While this may happen in some cases, it is easily avoided when one employs a proper and realistic focus and approach to growing in love of and devotion to God. As the *Catechism of the Catholic Church* states (in its very first teaching,) our one purpose in life is, "To know God, to serve God, and to Love God." If this is true (and it is), our intent should be to fulfill this purpose wholly and fully. Quite simply, this is the pursuit of perfection, and it is to be understood literally and in the absolute. We succeed in trying. We are, at our very core, absolute creatures. Ultimately, we will be rendered absolutely good and worthy of His paradise, or absolutely bad and unworthy of His paradise. Every material incident or action in our life leads us in one of those two directions. It can only make sense that our intent should be to only do what is good and pleasing to our Creator and Just Judge. Many important passages in Scripture affirm this, but perhaps none more so than Jesus's words, "Be perfect, as your Heavenly Father is perfect" (MT 5:48). The charge is clear. All my life I have been prone to the logic of absolute truth, even when I was unaware of that fact, or at least unable to articulate it. But now, fully aware of this reality, it simply makes sense.

I will not go further into the theology of perfection, whose pursuit, in practice, is enabled by His grace and our virtue. This theology is addressed in *Virtue* itself; indeed, it is *Virtue's* basis and central point. I mention this here to simply give an account of where my thoughts, based on my research, were leading. I am compelled to add, though, that I do not have a strong background in philosophy or theology, and am not naturally disposed to deep intellectual thinking. Still, while I struggled with some of the more esoteric writings on the subject, I nevertheless found myself, through His grace, growing in knowledge and understanding.

I began to write in earnest in January 2011. The initial working title was *Heroic Virtue.* St. Augustine coined that phrase in the fourth century to describe the extraordinary fortitude and faith of the Church's early martyrs. The term and concept has been adopted by the Church, and is applied to any situation in which an average person displays beyond-average virtue. My basic premise starting out was that to live a good and devout life in today's world one needed to employ an outsize, or heroic, virtue not just to win everlasting life, but *to simply be good.* After a time, though, I dropped the heroic aspect, and focused simply on a personal journey, through virtue, to God. It was around the time of this change that the form of my prose changed as well.

A prayerful rhythm began to emerge. In my writing day I began to relent, and to rely on Him more fully. Every day, at my desk under the skylight, the morning sun just overhead, I sought to do this not on my own, but led, as much as possible, by Him. I would type, sometimes, with my eyes closed, and while I never felt that the words came from any source but myself, I started to experience a certain *warmth* while the words took shape and meaning, a certain gratification—an acknowledgment, in a way, that what I was doing was right.

This was a time of great spiritual growth for me, a time when my perspective and, indeed, understanding of the world, was changing and deepening. Through the entire course of writing I was still studying the topic of virtue, drawing on the copious notes I had made, and constantly referring back to things I had read. My consumption of what I was reading, absorbing, and writing about was incredibly formative. I was on a quest, knowing, somehow, that when the book was over I would have figured *something* out; what that something *was* I could not put into words, except to say that it related to the obvious, to what the book was about: virtue. But virtue is not an end in itself; virtue, rooted properly, employed properly, can only lead to Him. I now realize that in writing about virtue as deeply as I was, I was seeking Him, and not merely to inform others. I was seeking Him in a way that I had wanted to for my entire life but up until that time I was too ignorant and too distracted and too self-obsessed. I was still all of these things, of course, but maybe just slightly less, and as soon as I opened that door, the good Lord stepped in, and started to lead me more directly, more fully.

I recognize now that I began, sometime that summer, to feel more *human*, in a way. Human in that best sense, in the sense that I understood, implicitly, where I came from. It was not that I understood any better *who* I was (though maybe I did,) but more importantly, *what* I was. And what that was, and is, is one of God's creatures. It's not that I ever doubted this fact, it just that what I sometimes took for granted became more *there*, more *present*. Once we are able to accept this most fundamental truth about our origins and place in the universe, once we acknowledge not just mentally but almost physically both His place and our place in the nature of things, then we begin to live it.

It was at this time that the world started to seem more full, yet, at the same time, if it makes any sense, emptier, more transient. I was drawn to those things that gave a sense of His presence both here and beyond, which, I see so clearly now, is practically everything. The Meditation of the Day in each day's *Magnificat* seemed so *full*, provided so much depth and insight, opened up new possibilities for me, new ways of understanding God, our world, our selves. These meditations, each just a few paragraphs long, are drawn from great writers, theologians, popes, priests, nuns and saints from over the centuries. I was particularly drawn to the meditations that, as I look back now, seemed to express the "experiential" nature of a relationship with Christ and His church. The words of one writer in particular, Caryll Houselander, spoke to me more deeply, or more consistently deeply, than all others. Caryll (1901-1954) was an English laywoman, artist, and writer. She was also, unsurprisingly, a mystic. I was also greatly influenced by excerpts from the writings of the great Dominican, Fr. John Tauler, another mystic, and from the French laywoman, writer and mystic, Madeleine Delbrel.

I must confess here that at some point that summer I actually looked up the word mystic for a definition (each of these contributors was identified as such). I hadn't been sure what it meant. Even after I read the definition it only made sense to me in an impersonal way. Though I understand now that mystical experiences vary (even as they all seem to possess a few basic common elements), my perception at the time was that mysticism was a "good day at prayer." I can say with conviction that, though these writers (and many others) influenced me deeply, mysticism was something that didn't practically equate with what I was writing, and I certainly did not connect it with anything I was feeling or experiencing. I continued on.

By the time fall arrived, I was seeking much more than a mere intellectual awareness. I was seeking a deepening relationship with God and with Jesus Christ, based in prayer. Though I am ashamed to admit this, I always had trouble praying the rosary. This trouble arose from more than just distraction. Though I never felt that Mary was the object of my prayer (a misconception of many), my difficulty was my own ignorance, my insufficient knowledge of the way in which Mary, given her exalted status, can lead us to the Father through her Son. (I am happy to note that I have since discovered this powerful grace). But still not ready at the time, I searched for a different devotion, something similar to the rosary. I found this in the Sacred Heart chaplet. I do not recall exactly how I came upon this sister devotion, except to say it was the result of an internet search. The prospect immediately appealed to me. I ordered a beautiful set of beads (there are a different number of beads on a Sacred Heart rosary than on a traditional rosary—thirty-three, representing the years Jesus spent on earth), and began to pray the chaplet daily, oftentimes several times a day. This I see as perhaps the greatest grace given to me in my prayer life, as the prayer spawned further devotion to the life-giving goodness He seeks to provide us through His most Sacred Heart. This devotion carried me through those early months of fall, bringing me closer to Him and providing solace and resolve as I neared the book's completion.

Two days before I would complete the book, on Monday night, October 31st, I laid awake in bed, disconcerted by a pain in my chest. I re-positioned myself, thinking it might be related to digestion, though the feeling was unlike any bout of indigestion I had ever had. My re-positioning did not make the pain go away. I considered telling my wife, who was asleep next to me, but did not, not wanting to alarm her with something I did not, somehow, perceive to be threatening. It went away after a time, and I slept. It was the first sign of His physical presence, a mere precursor.

And that brings me to that morning where I left off above—All Souls Day, November 2nd, 2011.

At my desk that early morning, under the skylight, sun above my head, I wrote, about love, that greatest virtue, and about true love's only fitting end. The writing flowed so freely. I let myself go, let myself write, feeling the end approaching. This was not a lot of words, a page-and-a-half at most, and this was not a lot of time, perhaps fifteen minutes. I hadn't sat down with the knowledge that the piece only required one page to completion, but I had known I was close. I wrote. I was led. I wrote. And then, then, at the very moment I typed the word that would complete the book, the Holy Spirit entered my body—my living soul —without warning and with such merciful fury that I was knocked to the ground in a fit of ecstasy. Wind, so strong, so powerful, blew through me, completely and utterly hollowing me out.

On my knees, I held on to my chair, knowing, somehow, from the very moment He had come that it was the Holy Spirit. I began to emit a horrendous noise, a noise resulting from my inability to contain what was being given, a noise I have since come to describe as a sort-of "honking exhalation." To put words to the overpowering, overwhelming joy of this mere drop of His presence would be impossible. To express, properly, what I was feeling, is *impossible*. What is even more astounding is that I knew, right then, while it was happening, that it was only a mere drop, a mere hint of Him. I knew this because I fought against it—this goodness, this grace, this most powerful ecstasy—absolutely enthralled by the euphoric goodness, but knowing that my soul couldn't handle all that was being given to me. I say *soul*, because this was distinct to me. It was my *very soul* that was so impacted; my soul conjoined, for now, to this body.

Still in the midst of this, I managed to get up. I stumbled into my bedroom, dropped to my knees and held on to my bed, the honking exhalation still coming, so loud now that my wife and children, two floors below me, came running to see what was happening. My wife came in first, the children right behind her, all of them clearly confused and concerned. Tears and tears of joy were flowing from me as I intermittently emitted the sound my daughter would describe later that day as that of a "dying cow"!

"It's the Holy Spirit. I finished my book. I'm fine." I said to my wife, repeatedly. I attempted to get up several times, laughing and crying joyfully, but was unable to do so. My wife managed to usher my children out. She closed the door and attended to me, and for the next few minutes I continued to experience the direct presence of the Holy Spirit inside me, gradually lessening; but even so, I was still barely able to stand, and still, intermittently, emitting that sound.

I can't even begin to describe what I was feeling emotionally and intellectually, except to say that it was all so blessedly *strange*. My wife was looking at me to make sure I was *truly* okay. I kept re-assuring her. I knew I was okay, but I was in shock. One distinct thought came to me at this time: *It's all true!*

"It's all true. Oh my God, *it's all true!*" I uttered, amazed.

I had never doubted in my life. Never. But never doubting is not the same thing as experiencing what one believes in faith. I had just experienced *God, Himself.* I was *still* experiencing Him. *Me!* I will say it again: it was so blessedly *strange*—so blessedly strange and confusing and wonderful and overwhelming.

And so there we were, my wife and I, in my office off my bedroom, both of us in shock now. I was still feeling the direct presence of the Holy Spirit, though intermittently and fading. My wife watched me, trying to talk to me, to understand what I was experiencing. What can be said in such a situation? She kept asking me if I was okay. I kept saying "Yes." We could hear our kids on the other side of the door, surely wondering what was going on. In trying to explain it to my wife—and, most definitely to myself—I said something along the lines of "He's happy with my work," thinking, initially, that His coming to me in this way—so definitive in its timing—was the result of His approving what I had written. "Amazing, amazing," I kept saying, along with other similar sentiments.

After about five minutes from His first coming, with the intensity of the ecstasy that I had experienced now fading, I began to feel utterly depleted and in a state of withdrawal; a confused and astounded withdrawal. I didn't know what to do with myself—stand, sit, cry, talk, pray.

Incredibly, and as *this-worldly* as this now seems by comparison, it was eight o'clock and my twins needed to be driven to school. Feeling exhilarated, astounded, shocked, overwhelmed, confused, affirmed, excited and many other things I composed myself as best I could, reassured my wife (repeatedly) that I was "okay," and then within five minutes was in my car, driving my kids to school.

+++

How do you make sense of this? How? We are given a *human* way of living. Direct experience with God in this way is outside the boundary of our normal human experience. What does one *do* when something so exceptional occurs? What?

Seriously, what?

Quite simply, I didn't know. It was as if, without warning, a spiritual meteor containing the answer—or at least the answer behind the answer—to every conceivable question had crashed through earth's atmosphere and struck only *me*. Furthermore, that spiritual meteor was invisible and the impact was only perceptible to *me*, and a part of me that cannot be physically seen. While my brain worked hard and fast to incorporate this knowledge and this experience into some type of frame of reference, and while my mind and soul worked together to marvel at and relish and recover from the sheer and overwhelming goodness of His presence—*His* presence. I will say it again, *His* presence, made one with me. God, Himself. *God!*

My goodness, God, Himself had not ten minutes prior infiltrated my soul, so thoroughly eclipsing my humanity, my understanding of life and the world, affirming everything I had ever believed, and while I so desperately wanted to figure out what *to do*, my four year-old twins intervened. There I was in the car with them and they wanted me to entertain them.

This was our daily custom. On the way out to school, I would warm them up for the day. They were still unsure of themselves, still becoming accustomed to these hours spent outside the home. We would chatter and sing. I would entertain them with thoughts of what we might do after school, about what their brother and sister and mother were doing right then. But their favorite daily routine was my asking them silly questions to loosen them up. So, what to do? In a very perfect way—and this was only pointed out to me much later by a learned Cistercian monk—I was doing, at that very time, *exactly* what He meant me to do. While I would have to struggle greatly over the next eight days in light of all that was happening to me, my earthly vocation as husband and father could never be disrupted—then, or since. So while the implications of my profoundly upended reality swirled in my head, I did the best I could to heed the immediate call of this earthly vocation. After seeing them into their classroom, I called my parents.

My father answered the phone. After a few pleasantries I said, "I finished my book." My parents knew that I was getting close to completing the book, and so this was not a surprise. But what I said next, of course, was. "Um, I had a mystical experience, an ecstasy," I said, and recounted what had happened. Properly conveying the otherworldliness of what I had experienced was impossible, though I tried.

What is a parent to say? A good parent would be both supportive and concerned, and my father was both of these. I repeated what I had said to my wife: that I believed God had somehow rewarded me for writing this book that professed utter devotion to Him through virtue. I am sure my father considered what I was telling him to be my feeling—at least in part— relieved and proud and gratified by accomplishing such a difficult task. And though I was feeling all of those things—it is by no means easy, seeing a book through to completion—what had happened to me was so clearly *not from me*, was so clearly outside the realm of regular religious experience, so clearly something that *could not be conjured*. I felt that he believed me, and though he never questioned the authenticity of what I had experienced, I am sure it was difficult, in a way, to hear. We talked for a few more minutes before hanging up.

Throughout the workday, my wife and I talked over the phone, recounting the episode. I have to mention, here, that my wife is Jewish. That she has indulged me in my devout faith would be an understatement. Even so, this type of mystical religious experience was very foreign to her (though, obviously, direct interaction with God is not unique to the New Testament). It wasn't exactly familiar for me either. For me, mysticism and ecstatic religious experience was the exclusive domain of medieval saints. Yes, there was Caryll Houselander, whose book, *Essential Writings*, I had recently purchased but hadn't read. Nevertheless, I had had no idea at the time about the nature of her experiences. In my attempts to put what I had experienced into context, I could only evoke St. John of the Cross, St. Teresa of Avila and St. Catherine of Siena, and even then I only had a vague idea about their experiences.

Aside from speaking to my wife, I simply proceeded through the day, picking my kids up and attending to other small responsibilities, and, despite my joy, still feeling awe over what had happened while also feeling incredibly affirmed in what I had written, I was, to a great degree, ill at ease, in a heavy state of withdrawal, not in the sense of needing some "fix," but, quite simply, spiritually, emotionally and intellectually *wiped out*. I had no inkling of what was to come, and couldn't really conceive of what "next" might be; I was just so overwhelmed—*the Holy Spirit had come to me*! If there was one consistent reflection throughout the day it was that realization I had had, that *It's all true*! *What He said, what scripture tells us*—*It's all true*! I marveled around that all day, shaking my head and laughing.

By evening I was able to reflect enough to know that my life would never be the same, that I was forever changed. I knew that further reflection was needed, but by and large I went to bed that night feeling that my life would return—in most ways—to normal the next day.

Day Two

Thursday, November 3, 2011

I awoke, on Day Two, with a feeling of comfort and good expectation, but still depleted and not quite myself. I said to my wife that morning, and throughout the next several days, "I'm still me," to reassure both her and myself; but I wasn't so sure.

I was anxious to get the kids off to school, knowing I had to shape the manuscript up in order to send it out, hopefully within a few weeks. Some stylistic issues needed to be addressed; the beginning portion of the manuscript needed to be brought in line with the rest of it. As I had mentioned, once I found my way, about a quarter of the way through the book, the form of the prose became more rhythmic, poetic, and I needed to bring that first quarter into the same rhythm. After I returned home from dropping my twins off at school, and with no little trepidation, I sat down at my desk in the office.

I started to read *Virtue* from the beginning. I initially liked what I was reading, but then, after a few pages, I wasn't so sure. The trepidation I had been feeling related to my expectations for the book, particularly in light of what I had experienced the previous day. What was it, I wondered, that I have written? Instead of trusting, I doubted. This is not to say that the work should have been perfect as it was—indeed, it wasn't. But the lack of trust, I would only recognize later, related to my expectations. If He is truly with us—and He is—He is with us always, in every moment, and if He chose to come to me in the way that He did, at the exact moment that He did—as I literally typed the period that would end the book—then He would ensure that the book would be what it needed to be. I knew this, implicitly, but feared the book perhaps wasn't meant to be at all, at least in a commercial sense. Maybe, quite simply, it wasn't good. Maybe His coming to me was only an affirmation of my effort, a consolation of sorts. To think that this might not have been enough hurts. There I was, a day removed from an ecstatic mystical experience (me—*me*!), and rather than taking the ultimate comfort in His having come to me in that most emphatic way, I was more concerned that my book would be "good" in the eyes of the world.

I read for a few more minutes and then stopped. I was having trouble concentrating. I had been a writer long enough to know I was in no state to be working on the book. I sat for a minute, just staring at my computer screen. I closed my eyes and breathed, feeling drawn to prayer. I started to have the desire to experience God again, and while I had no illusion that I was capable of *making* Him come to me, I simply wanted to be as close to Him in prayer as I could. I had, after all, been growing closer to Him throughout these months through efforts that I had made. Prayer had become more real to me, in a way. Perhaps for the first time in my life I had recognized a direct correlation between prayer and peace, between prayer and result, if that result was in accord with His will.

I left the office and went and knelt down at my bed, above which is another skylight. This is the spot where I have always started my writing day, on my knees, asking for His guidance and for the inspiration of the Holy Spirit that "I may find the words to praise the Lord, my God." As I got down on my knees, the sun above my head seemed so *present*. Throughout the course of writing *Virtue*, the sun had taken on special significance. I wrote about the sun and its power and symbolism extensively in the book, particularly in the first section (I am hardly the first to equate God with the sun, nevertheless it bears mentioning). With my Sacred Heart rosary in my hands, I began to pray.

Kneeling, praying, the sun above me, so bright, so warm, warm, I began to feel light, airy, I began to laugh lightly. I marveled at that, this laughter, this lightness. It continued, then joy, increasing, His presence, His presence, and then a quick, quick escalation of bright white light, warm, hot, coming so quickly, and then all at once, down into the top of my head and into my face, then into the rest of me, infiltrating me, enveloping me—and then nearly eviscerating me. Tears and tears, and I began to utter, repeatedly, and seemingly not from myself, *"Whatever you want me to do. Whatever you want me to do. Whatever you want me to do."* Upon reflection, I can say that these words seemed to come from my soul and not from my bodily intellect. My soul seemed to have an innate knowledge of *Him*. And in this knowledge, all it wanted to do was serve. I recognize, now, in this knowledge, a realization of our respective places in the universe; Creator and created; Ultimate Power and Might, and servile weakness. The brilliance of the light and the intensity of the warmth and joy and love became, after twenty seconds or so, overwhelming enough that I had to break away from it. It was so intense I thought that I might actually *die* were I to stay even a moment longer. This experience was so good, and so loving, but it was so overwhelmingly *powerful,* and so different from what I had experienced the day before. The experience was not a wholly affirming one in its particular ecstasy. *His* was a fearsome power. And it was even admonishing, in a way. It was this admonishment, but also the sheer force of this loving power, its ability to eviscerate me in the way that it did, the immediate heightened withdrawal it left, along with the instant recognition that "it had happened again," that suddenly made me very, very afraid. [I should mention here that it wasn't until two days later that I realized that, as opposed to the day before, which was a direct experience with the Holy Spirit, this experience was with God, the Father. More on that to come.]

I got up quickly and looked in the mirror on the wall beside me. I looked white, not un-humanly so, but paled, and wild eyed, and shaken. Once I was up, His presence was no longer directly with me in the same way, in the way of direct union, but I was elevated, charged, and feeling very much in a state of thankful grace, and this feeling, though very intense in the immediate aftermath of this experience and similarly intense at different points through the next week, did not leave me for the next seven days. As I will explain, this elevation would increase on Day Four and would render me, for days, absolutely ragged.

I called my wife immediately, but she didn't answer. I called my parents and talked to my mother. She seemed concerned, and incredulous. I tried to reassure her that whatever was happening, while disturbing, could only be good. She asked me questions about my health. I mentioned the presence in my chest from a few nights before—the precursor to all of this—and she was rightly concerned, perhaps thinking that I was delusional, or in the process of suffering a stroke or a heart attack, with blood flow impacting my ability to reason; any of the things any reasonable person would first consider. We hung up.

I paced. Sharon called. I said, "It happened again." And she said, supportive as always, and as blessedly affirming as always, "I knew it would." We talked.

It was from this point, from the late morning, as I dwelt in both in a state of grace and a state of disorientation—my purely human experiential foundation had been completely overturned—that an underlying feeling of dread came to me. This was no longer a "one-off," a situation where God might have somehow rewarded me because I had pleased Him with my book. I began to wonder what this was all about, and, more forebodingly, *what was going to happen next*. I began to want to have my former, merely devout, feel-good spirituality restored. I was afraid. His power had been so thoroughly eviscerating. I was so very afraid. For most of the next six days then, though drawn to prayer, I would not kneel down, fearing that He might come to me so forcefully again. Again, that power I had experienced was affirming but, in a very strong way, admonitory; not admonitory in a way that I felt I had done something wrong, but in the way of pure, inconceivable power. This power was loving, yes; but it was just so thoroughly *obliterating*.

As one might imagine, my mind churned the possibilities, reveled in the unlikeliness, and marveled at the otherworldliness of what I had experienced. But as much as I wanted to think of myself as "just myself," or "still myself," I wasn't. I wasn't still myself. I was, I knew, even before this second event, forever changed; but even that wasn't it. More expediently, right then and there, I didn't *feel* like myself. And not just from a standpoint of knowledge rooted in experience. I was elevated. This elevation was not euphoric (at least not all the time) but sentient. I felt. And what I felt I didn't necessarily *want* to feel, because what I felt or understood or experienced exceeded the realm of normal human experience, perception. I had an awareness that was hyper-acute. Unlike St. Catherine of Siena who, when approached by a person in a state of moral decay, could actually smell their putridness, my experience was more general, at least in the way that I related to individuals. I must say though that at times I had a much deeper sense of love and compassion for others than would normally be true. This was incredibly sustaining and helpful for me in my current life. But as for then, from that moment, I began to encounter the world differently, or more *feelingly*, both in a physical and a spiritual sense.

My experience at the school playground that afternoon exemplifies this well. It was tremendously difficult, feeling the way I did, "elevated," and having experienced what I experienced, and still having to be "Dad" to my children, and whatever other role I needed to play depending on whom I encountered. This contributed to the mental exhaustion I would suffer over the course of those days. But at the playground: it was after school and I was with my wife and kids. The playground was filled with children, and a dozen or so parents. I was off to the side, by myself, sitting on a rock, watching. As would be the case for most of the next six days, the day's light was unusually revealing, and had an uncommon hue. In this case, the light is perhaps best described as sepia-toned. The people all around me—children playing and their parents talking—were so very plainly "souls" inhabiting bodies. I had a tremendous feeling of love for these people. It was soothing and nice to feel this "unbiased" love for all of these "souls." And in terms of their being "souls," I do not mean to imply that I had a vision or visions or saw anything that anyone else could not see, I simply had cognition, understanding, seeing very plainly these fellow humans on the playground in their most elemental state. I had a direct sense of God's wholehearted desire that these souls should be with Him. This was beautiful, of course, but at this point I began to sense, also, that this would not necessarily be the case, that these souls would not necessarily be with him. I did not know if what I was recognizing related to anyone specifically on the playground—though my sense is that it did—but I knew that it was distinctly true in terms of the world in general. It made me sad, and marked the distinct emergence of my awareness of evil. It was from this point that I began to experience a creeping sense of evil's presence, both in the world in general and, even more disconcertingly, around me, as if lurking. This is aligned, I suppose, with the elevation I was experiencing, with my being neither quite here (in this world), nor quite there (in the world beyond), but having a sense for both. My experience confirmed the implication, stated in the prayer to St. Michael the Archangel, that evil spirits "roam the world seeking the destruction of souls," and it crossed my mind at the time that if I was some type of instrument of God, that I could become some type of target. This was *very* disconcerting. That thought lingered as I engaged, lightly, with my children and others before heading home. I discussed some of this, though not all, with my wife.

After dinner I decided to go to Eucharistic adoration at St. Louis church, a short walk from my house. It was dark out when I left the house. I felt uneasy heading out into the night, and as I walked I felt the distinct presence of evil, an intensification of what I had sensed earlier that day. This might be best described as a *palpable awareness*. I felt, in a way, watched. But it was even more than that. I had a direct sense of a malevolent presence *around* me, lurking. At this point, I was so mentally, physically and emotionally exhausted that this awareness was difficult to bear. I walked quickly, most of the way in the middle of the street where I felt safer, to get to the church.

Inside St. Louis, the adoration ceremony was intense and grace-filled and poignant as it had never been for me (I should say that I had only been to adoration a few times before). The gravity and clarity of the readings, my feeling, in a very real way, *His real presence*, not just in the monstrance, but simply *there*, among us, and my comprehension of the absolute profundity and goodness of the service itself--all of these things conspired to make this an other-worldly experience. Adding to this was my the onset of "points of light" in my chest and stomach. Much of this came in the form of what I have come to describe as a "holy crackling," little bursts of pleasureful pain. But there were also two distinct, and bigger spots, one on each side of my chest, just an inch or so in from each shoulder. The feeling in these two spots was more pronounced than the bursts—and whereas the bursts were just that, these two spots held their glorious pain, sometimes for a minute, sometimes for a few hours at a time (over the next week and beyond.) And all of this, the entire evening, took place under a most unusual yellowish and very revealing light.

After Adoration I walked home feeling safer and more assured, and wondering if—hoping that—that this would be the end of it.

Day Three

I woke up feeling more myself. I said my morning prayers, feeling God with me but in a conventional pre-November 2nd way. The nature of the day lent itself, at least at first, to little introspection. I had domestic responsibilities that required my attention. It was Friday, and so my twins did not have school. This was their first year of real schooling (pre-k,) and though I had much more time for myself and for writing, Fridays could still be a challenge. I very much enjoyed spending this time with them while my two older children were at school, but given all that had happened, on that day I simply wanted time to reflect, and to perhaps get back to editing *Virtue*. As a result, I was distracted and short with them. Though I always feel guilty in the aftermath of my being impatient with my children, there was a particular heaviness to my guilt that morning. I think it related to my feeling so unworthy of what I had experienced. This, what I was experiencing, was the domain of saints, not of ordinary, grumpy twenty-first century dads like me. God doesn't make mistakes, I knew, but nevertheless, I continued to reflect: *Why me?*

As the morning proceeded without event, I came to the conclusion, "Well, it's over." Still depleted and in a state of withdrawal, I was relieved to think that I would have my life as I knew it back. Somewhere inside, though, I longed, for at least the good and ecstatic parts of what I had experienced, but perhaps most of all for those points of light, the crackling; these otherworldly sensations, this pleasureful pain, that was so *good*, so *affirming*.

In a curious way, this whole notion of *what to do* had departed. Not that I, by any means, had any type of real answer, or that I had any conscious awareness that I was doing what I was meant to do. It was just that all this, as strange as it was, as otherworldly as it was, as life-altering as it was, simply *was*. I am not making light of it, I am simply saying I was just compelled to do what I, for the most part, would have done anyway; all the while, of course, wondering just what the heck was going on.

In the early afternoon, the intensity of my longing for Him, for His presence, returned in force. I believe the depth of this yearning emanated not from my intellect, which urged me otherwise, but from my soul, from my soul's *knowing* that He was so near, from an *awareness* that, despite my bodily ignorance and weakness, more interaction was possible. Over the course of these days (and subsequently) I began to appreciate a difference between the body's longings and the soul's. As Catholics, we are taught that as we ascend the spiritual mountain that leads to union with Him, we begin to live increasingly through the soul rather than the body. While I did not—and do not—consider myself to have progressed very far up that mountain, it is clear that through His grace, and despite my great impurity, my soul was, if not elevated, then more *present,* more *aware.* This awareness was made manifest by the very presence of the Holy Spirit inside me, or at least by the after-effects of such. It should stand to reason that given the immensity of God's total goodness and perfection, should we be visited thus, we cannot help but be changed, made different, at least for a time.

At this time, and for many months thereafter, I palpably felt this increased presence, and the resulting fruits accorded me. In Isaiah 11:2 we are taught about *The Seven Gifts of the Holy Spirit*: wisdom, counsel, understanding, knowledge, fortitude, piety, and fear of the Lord. Given my impurity, none of these were perfected in me, yet at different times it was clear that they were more deeply present in me. This was particularly noticeable after these eight days, when I had been brought back down from that sustained elevated state. There was a profound difference in me, and not just *because* of what I had experienced. I was the recipient of some, if not all, of those gifts of the Holy Spirit. Most obvious to me was a more acute understanding of *reality*, of Truth. I was, quite simply, a better person, at least a better *spiritual* person. The discord in this was that I was brought to this state abruptly, in an ecstatic mystical fashion, and not, more organically, as may be the case with those who have elevated themselves to a higher spiritual plane through their own hard spiritual work. This helped me to be better, and closer to Him, but the longstanding me—the impatient, grumpy, prideful me—still lurked just beneath the surface. From all I have read, I know that even the best of saints struggled to maintain their equanimity, their holiness, their purity, but I believe the difference here is that they were better at doing it on their own (with His help and grace, of course), whereas I had been plucked, given these fruits that were not necessarily commensurate with the spiritual work I had put in, and so at any waning moment I was prone to revert to that *real* me. And this, as I mentioned above, was the source of great, if not guilt, then discomfort rooted in the knowledge of my unworthiness.

But speaking to those gifts granted me, as I previously mentioned I have never been intellectually able to consume complex theology or deeply esoteric spiritual writing. That had changed, both during these eight days, but also for many months thereafter when nearly everything I read of a spiritual nature was so incredibly *weighty*, had so much meaning, so much portent—made so much sense. I understood what I was reading, but more than that I intuited it, I *felt* it. It was as if my protective human barrier, my dullness, my *unknowing*, had been peeled off and truth itself was revealed through this heightened ability to perceive. And it wasn't just spiritual writing, it was religious art as well. Sitting in the small but beautifully ornate chapel at the Monastery of the Precious Blood, where I had started attending morning Mass, after long periods of prayer after Mass, I would lean back and just *look*, marveling at the statues, the images of saints on the stained glass windows. Even the candles and the altar dressing that the sisters so lovingly changed daily and took great care of had an increased meaning. I was particularly drawn to the statue of the Blessed Virgin Mary, actually *feeling* her presence in that representation. She was not the statue, and the statue was not her, but she was so very much *present* in this representation. Again, as Catholics, we utilize signs and symbols and representations for the purpose of evocation. We do not worship *things*, we worship God, but God gives us things (nature) and the ability to create things from nature, and there is no greater constructed object than one that expressly attempts to evoke Him in His greatness, for the purpose of our imagining Him, sensing Him, evoking Him, and thus *knowing* Him. The most perfect evocation comes from inside us, of course; from that place that is our very soul; our very soul in communication with Him whether by His will in His coming to us, or by our appealing for His presence through prayer.

Finally, before I get back to that day, I must say that the most profound and most holy manifestation of the Holy Spirit inside me was on those several occasions in the ensuing months when I was given an awareness of Jesus's *real presence* in the Eucharist. This knowledge would be present, in some cases, from the moment I would wake up in the morning, an hour or so before heading to 7:00 a.m. Mass. On those days I would feel great anticipation as I walked from my house to the monastery, which was just a few short blocks away. The progression of the Mass was a crescendo, with each step heightening my anticipation as I struggled, sometimes unsuccessfully, to control my tears and my trembling, as I went forward to receive Him. There was one time, even, when I though the priest might ask me to move on, given my near inability to open my mouth to receive Him.

But returning to that day, when this was all so very new and confusing to me, and returning to my soul's longing for His presence despite my withdrawal, at around three o'clock I walked with my twins over to pick up my two older children at their school, which is just across the street from our house. Crossing the street, and with my twins in tow, I reached into my pocket for my Sacred Heart Rosary and began to silently pray the Sacred Heart chaplet. Immediately I felt a stirring in my chest, and a warming sensation. Within seconds those two sharp points on either side of my upper chest near my shoulders reappeared. I was also instantly elevated, *brought up*. This all happened within perhaps thirty seconds.

As I walked and prayed a sense of great love came over me, inspiring, in turn, a great love for those around me. This is telling, I believe, in that this love went *beyond* me, beyond any personal satisfaction or gratification that one might ordinarily derive in simply *being* loved. This love inspired in me *love for others*, for those who were simply in my eye's view. This was remarkable, and as I proceeded to walk, I began to detect "souls" in much the same way as on the playground the day before; people appeared very much the way they always do, but I was given an *awareness* of their very essence. And while this awareness was similar to what I had experienced the day before, my *state* was different. It is hard to adequately describe the elevation I experienced, except to say that I felt *brought out* from myself, separate, yet so whole, and so lovingly, lovingly euphoric, so lovingly, lovingly, *warm and loved.* This was a stark contrast to both the overpowering wind of the Holy Spirit blowing through me on the first day, and the almost unbearable love and light and power of God the Father on the second day. (It is important to note, again, that it wouldn't be until the two days later that I would understand that Day Two's experience had been with God the Father.)

There are several pick up points at the school, depending on the grade of the child. Our pick up point was inside the school in a common area known as "the bricks." When my twins and I walked in, my wife was already there waiting. She smiled at me. There was so much to be said. But obviously this was not the time. While my twins hugged and talked to her, I took a few steps away, to consider what was happening with me. I marveled at what I was feeling, and realized, very deeply, that it was Christ's presence. It was so different from what I had felt on those previous two days, so much more loving, more peaceful, but most of all more loving, loving, *pure love.*

Soon, the doors opened and out poured the children, a beautiful, noisy, multi-colored array. One of the great aspects of this school is its diversity, a population in which my children are a minority. When my own two children emerged I hugged them and, as we often did, my entire family hung around for a bit, my wife and I chatting with some parents while our kids played with their friends around us. It was difficult to contain the joy I was experiencing, though I was still able to focus. One of the women we were talking to was discussing a hardship she was experiencing and I felt a deep and loving empathy for her. The level of this love and empathy went *far beyond* what I would normally feel. This, I believe, was the love and empathy of Jesus, Himself, who was so very present in my soul. The points of light continued to lightly pierce me, and the "holy crackling" continued. I was amazed, and awestruck. It was soon time to go, but I was reluctant, not wanting what I was experiencing to end.

We had arranged previously that my wife would take my two daughters to a doctor's appointment, and that I would go home with the boys. I was disappointed about this because I wanted to be with her, to share the warmth I was feeling, if not verbally (I was still wary, still unsure of what she might think) then simply by being together. But we had our responsibilities. We went our separate ways.

As I was walking home with the boys, I continued to feel the warmth and euphoria and love inside me, and it was, in fact, growing even stronger. I was thinking "here we go again," and though I was unsure of where "here" was (I wasn't yet separating my experiences), it bears repeating that what I was experiencing was starkly different from the experience of the first two days. Whereas those two experiences had been overwhelming and overpowering and immediately depleting, I wanted more of what I was then experiencing, this pure warmth, this calm, this peace, this love.

When we got inside the house, I stopped for a minute in the kitchen and could feel the love grow even stronger inside me, completely uplifting me, my soul inside me. My boys went upstairs to play on the computer, and I followed them a moment later. When I arrived at the top of the stairs, I paused outside my son's room. There is a sticker for *The Presence,* a local Catholic radio station, on his door. On the sticker is a rendering of the Eucharist and dynamic rays of light emanating from it. I was drawn to it and touched it and found myself staring at it for a moment, the warmth growing even more intensely inside me, pulsing, pulsing, and then my eyes were drawn to the floor of the bedroom, where the sun was shimmering onto the floor, shining in an assortment of dynamic rays, as if mimicking the shining off the blessed Eucharist on the sticker, but supernaturally, and so much brighter, faster, shinier. I became even more filled, and warm, warm. My breath grew heavy. Heavy, heavy breathing and warmth, warmth, as I watched the floor and the dynamic light show that was taking place before me. My chest was so warm. The rays were so incredible, *so fascinating,* glittering—but with God's real light from the sun. My boys called me to their game and I pulled myself away, reluctantly. I saw to their needs and returned to my son's room and to the floor, where the flickering was still going on, though less intensely. Although I pleaded for it to continue, after ten seconds or so it stopped entirely.

The warmth and the love and the euphoria continued for a time but over the course of an hour waned entirely, leaving me again depleted. This depletion was so taxing, so draining, so confusing. My confusion was not in the way of not understanding, but was more of a mental tiredness that made it difficult to engage. With the boys occupied by the computer, I simply walked about the house, ruminating on all that was happening.

When my wife and daughters arrived home an hour or so later I put on my best face. I didn't mention anything to my wife about this latest experience. I was feeling embarrassed and slightly ashamed. These are incredible sentiments, as I look back at it. Yes, it was God, Himself revealing Himself to me and one would think that that would be "enough," a sort of ultimate affirmation of, well, *everything*. But there was such a heaviness to all this. There were my own feelings of inadequacy, of course, of my being unworthy, but also impacting my human feelings was my human inability to handle such power and grace. And not to mention my confusion; *this was not normal!* I was unable to place what I was experiencing into any proper frame of reference. My pervasive feeling had gone from *"This is unspeakably amazing,"* to *"Why is this happening to me, and when is it going to stop?"* It can perhaps be understood, then, the tremendous feeling of aloneness that began to come over me. Adding to the aloneness was my being downright afraid. I still possessed a waxing and waning awareness of evil around me, and was overwhelmed by this general state of *knowing*, of *elevation*. At the same time, I understood myself to be in a state of grace. I frequently reminded myself what I had said to my mother the previous day, "This is from God, and so it can only be good." While I took great comfort in this, what I was experiencing was still very much to handle. If there was one person that I needed, it was my wife. She has always been my earthly refuge. She is so good and accepting and loving, and people are drawn to her because of the warmth and vitality and understanding she exhibits and exudes. People—friends and strangers alike—will often say to her, "Why am I telling you this?" amazed at what she lovingly draws out. My house is a magnet for so many of the underprivileged neighborhood kids, and that is largely because of her, because she so selflessly gives them attention. But what I was experiencing was so far beyond the realm of what was normal that I was afraid she would not continue to understand or accept it, or that, even worse, she would be put off by it. My parents' tepid and polite reaction over the previous two days had made me feel less than understood and embraced (and I can't blame them—this type of experience is so categorically extraordinary), and this made me wary of my wife's potential response to this ongoing phenomena that was impacting me—and thus her and the rest of the family.

But, I have never been able to keep anything from my wife. After dinner, when the kids had gone off to their games and lives, at the right moment, while we were clearing the table and doing dishes, I told her. As always, as she has always been, she was smiling and wonderful and wholly supportive. She is heaven-sent. Truly.

As I spoke to her, the warmth from earlier that day re-emerged and grew in my chest. The little points of light pulsed and crackled, the big points by my shoulders returned. We talked about how amazing this all was. And we talked some more. And then we went about our evening routine, engaging the kids and getting them ready to turn in for the night. I went to bed that night amazed and filled and jittery and thankful and unsettled and, perhaps most of all, hopeful that this would be the end of it.

Day Four

This was not to be the end of it. I woke up the next morning, Saturday, Day Four, sensing the strong presence of the Holy Spirit inside me—a wholly good and affirming feeling—and I felt very much in a state of grace. This grace was not euphoric, but had rendered me "spiritually elevated." But while I felt good and hopeful, I most definitely did not feel like "me." I would later recognize that I had passed into a place where the fluctuating otherworldliness of what I had been experiencing was now (at least temporarily) permanent. This, right then, and for the coming five days, was to become my constant reality, an existence "not quite here, and not quite there."

This elevation was characterized by a heightened, mostly spiritual, *awareness*. Objects were still objects, just more vividly so, and people were so *very, very much more*. At times, it was as if all manner of existence around me had been laid bare, reduced to its most basic meaning; and thus, elevated incomparably. Life—from the grand to the minute—was so saturated with meaning, with portent, with depth. All that was *true* had simply become so very *present*. I wrote about

51

this elemental understanding of the world in *Virtue*, but there it was treated in a more theoretical sense, or at the very least in a way mediated by writing. Now this theoretical intuition had become *my reality*, my lived experience. In this life we are necessarily veiled, and for good reason. First, God wants us to come to Him on our own. If He makes Himself known so explicitly (as He was doing to me at that time) we have really no choice but to acknowledge Him for who He is and thus believe. Second, there is an intensity to our existence that, more fully experienced, overwhelms the senses. Because of the depth of our existence, everything has meaning (and, again, particularly ourselves). Surrounded as we are by this endless depth, should we be constantly *aware* as such, intuiting and contemplating and recognizing and seeing—it is all just too much. Throughout those days, I avoided *depth* as often as I could. Even a casual glance from a stranger was so engrossing, so *filled*, so fit to be endlessly parsed and considered. I was forced, in many ways, to dull myself. As I previously mentioned, I was actually afraid to even pray to Him at that time, fearing absolute evisceration by His loving Truth. I talked to Him, but would not get down on my knees. I recognized all that was happening as being explicitly good; it was just simply *too much*, and this had a physical manifestation as well. All this knowledge, all this essence, all this stimuli was so thoroughly *exhausting*, of course, but at times I would feel *raised up*, in a way. Not in an ethereal sense (though that was to come), but something more contradictory, as a sort of "floating heaviness." The heaviness, I believe, related to the imperfection of my soul, but also to the very *presence* of my body. I was still very much there, very much *present* in the world. I was still aware of all that had been *me* up to that point, indeed, still *was* me, yet this whole new level of *being* had taken over, and it was difficult to bear.

As I lay in bed, my wife asleep beside me, I considered all this (or the part of it I could then understand). I knew that what was happening was mystical, but in attempting to put this into context I was really only able to evoke, again, the names of some of those well-known medieval mystics, and, just vaguely, a few others; but really, what did I have in common with any of them? Again, this was thoroughly disconcerting. Though I felt blessed by His presence, I simply wanted this to end and to have my previous life back. I was still incredibly depleted, as if I hadn't slept at all, and I began to wonder if I would *ever* feel like me again. I envisioned a whole day of having my four young children about, each of whose needs demanded attention, a whole day of interaction with the world, a world that had become so much more intense, so much more *real*, yet so different from what it had been up to that point.

There was also the question of the book. I have always been a motivated writer, and never liked missing a day of writing. I often write six days a week. I very much wanted to get back to *Virtue*, to polish it and send it out. This, again, I recognize now, makes perfect sense. To be experiencing God as I was, and to not simply lay down on the ground like a spiritual sponge, but to continue to exist as He wanted me to, and not just as husband and father, but also as *writer*, is so obvious to me now. In any event, at the time I was also, as one might imagine, greatly intrigued by what the fate of the book might be. His coming to me so dramatically, so forcefully, after I had literally typed the period that would end the book, was so emphatic that I couldn't help but think, "What is it that I've written?" My few glimpses of the book since finishing it, however, gave me less than full confidence that I had written some type of groundbreaking or deeply incisive book. This only inspired more confusion, and even guilt; I believed that what I was experiencing did not necessarily match up with what I had written, and it certainly did not match up with my perceived state of holiness.

Lying there, feeling all that I was still feeling, the doubt, but also His *very presence* inside me in such a physical way, I began to wonder what, exactly, His plan for me was. This was all so unprecedented, so strange, so exceptional and so life-altering that I began to wonder if I was, in some way, "anointed." My thoughts were not on the order of a delusion of extreme holiness or mission, but more in the way of, "If He is doing this for me, what does He *want* from me?" Given my general state of withdrawal, of uneasiness, of my waxing and waning awareness of "evil" around me, it was not a comforting feeling.

I had the urge, for the first time, to speak with someone. My inclination was to speak with Fr. Paul, a priest from my local cluster. Fr. Paul is not a priest with whom I had a relationship, though I was quite familiar with him given his residency at St. Louis, where I went frequently for Mass during the week. I thought it was unusual that I would be drawn to speak with Fr. Paul—I had never spoken with him before, and I knew other priests in the cluster better—but I felt the Lord was leading me in that direction. I did not know when or how I would approach him, but decided that when the time came it would be revealed to me.

In any event, the day had now fully dawned, and my children had joined us, one by one, in bed. I opened up the shades and the light streamed in, and there we were, the six of us for a blessed (if somewhat crowded) few minutes, goofing and talking about the day. It was comforting in its normalcy, and we all soon headed downstairs together to engage in our usual Saturday morning routine.

When we got downstairs my wife inquired as to how I was feeling. I did not go into much detail, intent as I was to, insofar as it was possible, try to *ignore* what was happening. I say this in the sense that I simply had to go on with my life. This may sound rather obvious, but there I was, on the verge of what felt like a burgeoning crisis. It was a divinely inspired crisis, of course, but nevertheless, what I was experiencing was so consuming, so outside the realm of normal human experience. The difference was that most crises have an endpoint, or a solution. What was the solution to this?

And so after engaging for a while downstairs, and in an attempt to find an answer to the crisis through what had brought me there, I returned to my office and to *Virtue*. I began reading but it was difficult to concentrate. The sun overhead was so *powerful*, and I was so very much in the midst of this elevated state that prevented me from focusing. I soon decided I couldn't look at the manuscript right then, which was incredibly disappointing. One of my children soon came in and there I was, brought out, necessarily, (there are no coincidences), with the rest of the day before me.

+++

Thankfully, the day proceeded without a major event, along the lines of the previous three days. I continued to operate as a husband, a father, a neighbor in very much the same way as I always had, though what was going on inside me, and in terms of my own reality, was very different. It was not easy to maintain both fronts. In addition to the "eternal truths" that had moved to the forefront of my consciousness, the same questions rotated in my head all day: *What* was this? *Why* was this? *When* will it end? My elevation throughout the day never subsided. And never leaving me were those two powerful points on either side of my chest just inside each shoulder. I can again describe the feeling as a sort of glorious pain, a pain that pulses in the way of a *living presence*, a *knowing*. It felt very, very good. And it was remarkably affirming, particularly given my general disorientation. But it also begged a question. Given the marked difference between the way these two points felt, and the less intense—yet no less sublime—"holy crackling" and "points of light" I experienced in my stomach, chest and, occasionally, back, I wondered about their seemingly overt significance. At the time, I thought these two points might relate to the Holy Spirit. In making the sign of the cross ("In the name of the Father, and of the Son, and of the Holy Spirit") I noticed the two points coincided with the very same spots at which I would say "...and the *Holy Spirit.*"

That afternoon, these points and other physical manifestations of His presence intensified when I found myself inside a Congregational Church for an Autumn Bazaar. I was there with my family for this neighborhood event we attend every year. We ambled about as always, looking at the homemade knick-knacks, sampling food, talking to neighbors and friends. This was a challenge at times, but I persisted. Again, I was elevated throughout, but when I walked into a large sanctuary-type room adorned with beautiful stained glass, the "holy crackling" intensified dramatically. (This would happen for many months thereafter, when I would either come into contact with very holy people, situations, or "things" (even as I approached the spiritual books section at Borders)). But there in the sanctuary, I was surprised, in a way, or at least caught off guard. As a devout Catholic, I have always been at least subconsciously (at times, overtly) dismissive of my more progressive Christian brethren.

My belief in the primacy of Catholic doctrine and dogma has not changed, but this experience was enlightening. I can simply say that I felt, mystically, God's presence in that place of worship, and it was really, really good. While I would never have doubted that He could be so present in such a place, having an experiential understanding versus an intellectual one was enlightening.

Shortly thereafter it was time to go. We emerged back into the day, the November sun fading. Back at home, day soon turned into night, and I felt hopeful. Despite my ongoing elevation and the depletion and exhaustion it wrought, and despite my ongoing awareness of that lurking malevolence, given the lack of a major encounter that day (along the lines of those previous three days) I could hope that my normal reality would soon be restored, perhaps after a night of sleep.

But as I would learn from the very moment I woke up the next morning, Day Four was just an interlude.

Day Five

Sunday, November 6, 2011

Sunday, November 6, Day Five, was the most dramatic, in many ways, of all these eight days. I awoke that morning extremely elevated. From the moment I first awoke, I wanted to see Fr. Paul that day. It was a specific recognition, unlike the day before, and thus I took it as inspired. I had plans to be at the Cathedral of the Immaculate Conception, the seat of the Bishop of Portland, and our regular church, at nine that morning for a catechism meeting. I got out of bed and looked on-line at the cluster bulletin to see where Fr. Paul would be that day. I saw that he was celebrating the eight o'clock Mass at the Cathedral that morning. This was highly unusual. Fr. Paul infrequently celebrates Mass at the Cathedral, being the full-time chaplain at Maine Medical Center, residing at and saying Sunday and weekday Mass, at St. Louis. In fact, in my eight years of Sunday Mass at the Cathedral, I had never known Fr. Paul to say Sunday Mass there—at least I had never been to one of his Masses. I took his presence there that morning, and at a time when I would be arriving (and he would be leaving) as a further sign that I was indeed meant to speak with him. I intended to catch him after his Mass was over, and just before my nine o'clock meeting.

As I had said, I was extremely elevated from the moment I woke up. This elevation was different. It was intensely grace-filled, and entirely positive. It was not tinged with the trepidation or depleted confusion or emotional ambivalence or fright resulting from an awareness of evil that had characterized my elevation to this point. I was feeling stronger. And I was *very* euphoric; filled with a tremendous feeling of love, but most of all, grace. As I went about my early morning routine the euphoria was only growing and intensifying.

With my family downstairs, I was drawn back to my bedroom and office. Alone in my bedroom, trying to figure out what I should do with myself, I saw that the light streaming in through the skylight was impossibly white and brilliant and I was becoming filled, even more, and ever more, *filled*. Euphoric. Absolutely euphoric. Euphoric in a way that I can perhaps best describe as *spiritually floating*, a pulsing, surging goodness, a satisfaction based in an intense feeling of love, and even holy portent. There was none of the heaviness from the previous day. I went to my desk and sat down and started to read *Virtue* on the computer, editing lightly, and feeling as if a golden hand was guiding me. After a few pages, I couldn't contain myself. The power of the euphoria was so intoxicating I needed to get up, move about.

My wife soon came upstairs and into the bedroom to discuss our morning plans. She noticed right away the extraordinary brightness of the light in the room. We marveled at it together. This was so wonderful to me, because she, too, was witnessing something supernatural. And it was interesting, a signal that, at least right then and there, what was transpiring was not for me alone. It helped me to have her to see this physical manifestation of something so astonishing. It was still just the sun, but it was so very, very *bright*. It wasn't that I ever felt that she doubted me or doubted what I was experiencing—she had witnessed my "honking exhalation" several days prior, after all—but for her to see this tangible proof that God was continuing to reveal Himself was amazing and affirming and comforting. Of course, at the time, I only considered what all this might mean for *me*, and not for her; but that is her story to tell.

As I dressed and got ready to head down to the Cathedral, this great light all around us, I explained to her what I was experiencing, how the euphoria was increasing, and how much more intense and grace-filled I felt as compared to the previous days. I also told her that I had realized something for the first time that morning: that I now understood the experiences of those first three days to have been Trinitarian in nature. I had known right away, on that first day that it was the Holy Spirit who had come to me. Not only was I given the knowledge from the very moment of His coming, but the manner in which the Spirit came, the way in which the Spirit had blown through me, through my soul, was an undeniable mark. I explained that on the third day it had been clear that Jesus's presence had been with me and in me. He had come when I began to pray the Sacred Heart rosary, and He revealed Himself to me in the loving—*so very loving*—warmth and satisfying goodness that had filled me while I watched the rays of light, as if emanating from the monstrance, twinkling supernaturally on the floor in front of me. This association is also undeniable. But it had only occurred to me that morning that on that second day it had been God, the Father, who had come to me, down in through the top of my head, into my face, my body, so powerfully and yet, of course, still so lovingly. If there was one overriding characteristic of that second experience, however, it was the sense of absolute, even terrifying power of the Father. As I mentioned, I had had to pull myself away from His power and might for fear that I might actually *die*, my tiny and pitiful soul so incapable of handling the all-powerful, all-mighty goodness of Him. These words I write are so unsatisfactory in attempting to express what I experienced, the absolutely eviscerating and annihilating heat, power, goodness and love that was some small part of His presence. And, as I said previously, the loving admonishment that was also so present. As I reflect on it now, I do believe admonishment is apt. It is clear that, for some reason, I had found favor with God, and this was why He was coming to me in this way, but as He brought me into His presence I believe this admonishment was reflected in the simple impurity of my soul. It was not His anger that I felt, but, perhaps, more of a loving chiding. And my soul itself, as I also mentioned previously, knowing its place, had inspired me to utter, "Whatever you want me to do, whatever you want me to do..." Contrition, perhaps, but also recognition of our true respective places.

As always, my wife was good and understanding and supportive. She was very much effected by my words and by what was occurring. This was, again, comforting. But it was time for me to leave. We arranged to meet at the Cathedral for our usual ten o'clock Mass. As I got ready to leave I felt, absolutely, on a mission.

In the car, driving down Congress Street, it was as if I was floating, floating, and as if I was upheld and guided by angels. The light, the warmth, the overwhelming, ethereal, loving goodness. Running through my mind, of course, were many questions: What was happening? Why was I so elevated? What did He have in mind for me? Where was this all heading? I had been asking these questions for days now, but this was different. I possessed a certain sense of conviction, emanating, most definitely, from this ascendant and purely blissful and prolonged ecstasy I was experiencing. And I was both excited and relieved by the prospect of speaking with Fr. Paul. I thought that some or all of my many questions would be answered. Despite my conviction, though, there was still an underlying fear of the unknown. There was absolutely no blueprint that I was aware of for what might come next. My living and conscious ecstasy was so transcendent that one can perhaps understand my feeling, in a very deep way, of being "anointed." Given the way I was feeling, I was no longer so sure that whatever He had in mind for me was either "small" or related only to myself. Overwhelming.

I pulled into the parking lot just before nine, my heart and my soul *leaping*. I saw that Mass was over, the parking lot mostly empty. I walked into the church and into the sacristy, expecting to see Fr. Paul. I did not see him. Three men were standing there, though, one I knew by sight, one I knew personally, and one I didn't know at all. I said, "Is Fr. Paul here?" The man I knew only by sight said to me, "He's waiting for you at Maine Med."

Huh? I thought.

He's waiting for me?

Attempting to recover, I said, "He's not here?"

"He's waiting for you at Maine Med," the man said again.

His words hit me.

The way in which the man's mouth had moved, his affect... it was clear he had no idea what he was saying. The Lord had put the words in his mouth.

I hadn't told anyone, except my wife, and not even an hour before, that I was intending to speak with Fr. Paul. Fr. Paul could not have possibly known I was coming. Fr. Paul didn't know my name, and neither did this man. I hadn't even mentioned my name. I had simply asked, "Is Fr. Paul here?"

It was like something from the Bible. I was floored.

I believe the man said, "He's waiting for you at Maine Med," a third time, at which point I just stepped back into the church from the sacristy and felt my soul soar even higher. So much levity, so much ethereal levity, so absolutely taken and infused with wonder and shock and awe. I nearly burst into tears.

As I stood just outside the sacristy, attempting composure, I said to myself, *He's waiting for me? Did I just hear that? Is that what he just said? He's* waiting *for me?* It was almost too much to bear. What did this mean? What did all this mean? Did Fr. Paul have instructions for me? What was I going to be asked to do?

I walked toward the back of the church, feeling my very soul inside me, zooming, floating, zooming, my mind racing. I came upon a group of a half-dozen or so Vietnamese men and women praying the rosary in their native tongue. Their method is sing-songy, and their voices together held such sweet, sweet appeal. I stopped for a moment, experiencing the sustained presence of the Holy Spirit swirling above them and about them as they prayed. This was incredible. Incredible, this physical manifestation of His presence in their evocative prayer. This very *affirmation* of the power of prayer. Incredible, His letting me in this way, His giving me this knowledge. I continued on to the back of the church, marveling at all I was witnessing. I could hardly contain myself. It was as if at any moment I would just fly away.

I soon realized, however, that it was now past nine, and I walked back toward the front of the church and out of the side doors and across the parking lot on my way to the school where the religious education coordinator would be. A car with a *The Presence* bumper sticker slowly drove past me. The way I was spiritually floating, and the way in which the light of the day was coming to me, so orange and bright, and the way in which the car seemed to be moving so slowly, I was given to feeling that I was very much being escorted. This feeling would continue, and would be marked by another, even more marked event, which I will get to in a bit.

Into the school. I found the classroom, feeling self-conscious in my euphoria, in my state of being "not quite here, not quite there"—but at this point, much more "not quite here"—yet needing to be grounded, to at least appear to be "fully here" in order to interact with others, to take care of these few routine tasks. I spoke with the religious education coordinator briefly, and then, inside the classroom I spoke with a woman, a mother of many children, who was homeschooling her little ones. My interaction with her was so love-filled, so full of trust.

I managed to get through the relatively short meeting, in which we were given instruction about the catechism materials, the timing of events, etc. It all seemed so very *good*. After the meeting, I returned to the church to wait for my family and ten o'clock Mass, the words, *"He's waiting for you at Maine Med,"* churning and churning in my head.

It was still a bit early and my family had not yet arrived. I sat in our usual spot. As I sat and looked about, fixated on the Biblical scenes depicted in the stained glass, *feeling them*, I also felt the unadulterated euphoria beginning to wane, opening the door to trepidation.

He's waiting for me?

What was I going to be asked to do? I was afraid. This—all of this that I was experiencing—had quite simply gone beyond any conception I had not just of what I may encounter in my life—*but in the life of anyone who had ever lived!* It was, in the very truest sense, surreal. Surreal, yet I was so fully aware that it was *actually happening*. And whatever it was—this; this whatever it was—was happening to me. This husband and father. God had infiltrated my life so physically and so powerfully and—most of all—so *disturbingly*. And it was growing more disturbing by the minute. Over the last few hours this entire experience had gone from one of mind-numbing but grace-filled improbability to (all of these things remaining) now, in light of Fr. Paul "waiting for me" at Maine Med, to an outright feeling of having been *anointed* for something, feeling *chosen*. The questions repeated: What was it? What was I going to be asked to do? What had I been chosen for? The possibilities surged, most of them negative; or, at least, dire and unsavory. Suffering? Humiliation? Attack? Death? I was still extremely elevated, still feeling His presence, still feeling the warm glow of His goodness, but this was all so very much.

Finally, my family showed up. Seeing them walk into the church, seeing my wife's welcome face, I was soothed. She looked at me expectantly, clearly wondering if I had already spoken with Fr. Paul. Just as Mass was beginning I was able to tell her, briefly, what had happened. I told her about the man's words, "He's waiting for you at Maine Med." She smiled and even laughed a little—no doubt at the outright ridiculousness of what was taking place. Needless to say, for where I was at in my mind, this was consoling. I even managed to laugh a little myself. Now that I think back on it, that she was so *there* with me, indulging every single aspect of what I was experiencing, while not surprising, is so incredibly and unequivocally trusting and loving. She is amazing.

Mass couldn't be over fast enough. I wanted to see Fr. Paul. I wanted to have at least some inkling of what my fate would be, of what all this might be about. When Mass was over I told my wife I was heading directly to Maine Med, and I left. Though Maine Med is in my neighborhood, instead of going home and walking over I drove directly there. I parked and began walking to the main entrance. At about a half a block from the entrance I noticed a priest approaching the door from the opposite direction and from approximately the same distance. I did not recognize this priest. I wondered who he was; was he here to see *me*? We arrived at the door at the exact same time. I recognized this as being no coincidence, that I was being escorted, again, through my day, and now specifically into this impending meeting with Fr. Paul. The priest, however, didn't really take notice of me, and I opened the door for him and said, "I am here to speak with Fr. Paul," thinking, perhaps, he would, if not know me, then he would know Fr. Paul.

"Who?" he said.

"The chaplain."

He said something along the lines of his not knowing Fr. Paul, and he passed through and on his way. I was perplexed, and lightly embarrassed, but continued on.

Though I had been in the hospital many times before (three of my four children had been born there), I didn't know where the chaplain's office was. I went to the information desk, found out where to go and went, the euphoria again building. I was feeling nervous and intensely *interested* in what was going to happen. I was going to, I thought, at least have some type of answer to this *crisis*. I should mention that even though the outright, feeling-as-if-floating euphoria had departed, the extreme elevation had never left. I was *very*, *very* elevated still. This elevation was grace-filled and much more intense than at any time during the eight days.

I got off the elevator. The whole area was extremely quiet. It was a largely administrative wing, and it was Sunday. Fr. Paul's office was a short walk. The door to his office was closed. I knocked, but there was no answer. The chapel was right across the hall. A sign outside it announced that a Catholic Mass was soon going to be celebrated, so I knew that Fr. Paul would arrive shortly. I paced and paced, turning the corner, turning back, pacing, walking, and then after about fifteen minutes, finally, from the end of a long hall I heard footsteps. Fr. Paul turned the corner and I walked toward him, seemingly in slow motion. I looked for recognition from him as he approached. There was none. He would have walked past me, if I hadn't said his name.

"Fr. Paul?"

"Yes?" he said.

"My name is Andrew McNabb and I need to speak with you."

There was no recognition from him as to who I was. He certainly hadn't been "waiting" for me, but I didn't have time to even consider that, and furthermore, it didn't matter. I simply needed to speak to him, urgently. He said that he needed to prepare for Mass, but that I could speak with him after Mass if I could wait. I told him I had been at the Cathedral Mass at ten o'clock that morning, but that I would certainly wait. He looked into the chapel while I stood in the hall. I could see that no one was there yet. He said that even if no one else showed up he would still have to say Mass.

He went into his office to prepare for Mass and I went into the chapel and sat down. With no other chairs filled, I immediately thought, "Oh my God, he's going to be saying Mass for me alone." It was another sign, I thought, that I was in some way *anointed*. It was incredible, and daunting. I envisioned myself sitting there, the holy sacrifice of the Mass being consummate for *me alone*. It was only a minute, though, before two people came in and sat down, and I began to feel less exalted, less anointed. I felt foolish, in a way, for having had that thought in the first place. Another few people arrived and Mass began, and as I sat it was difficult to pray, difficult to focus. I in my head I went over what I would say to Fr. Paul, and I tried to think what his reaction might be. Mass passed surprisingly quickly.

After Mass, Fr. Paul welcomed me into his office. He closed the door and we sat down. The feeling of expectation I had, of impending relief, was incredible. I told him I needed to speak to him about something I had been experiencing, but that I needed to preface this by giving him some background on me. I wanted to give him comfort that I was not some crazy who had wandered into the hospital looking for attention. I gave him a copy of my story collection (as evidence of my being a writer), told him about my family, my various forms of involvement in the parish, and how he might recognize me from Adoration or from my attending some of his weeknight Masses at St. Louis. He was polite.

And then I sat for a minute, composed myself and proceeded to tell him all of what I have written above, through tears and overwhelming emotion. Fr. Paul was very good, and very understanding and very compassionate—and very matter of fact. I had half-expected him to pull a red phone out of his drawer for a direct dial to the Vatican, "*He's here. He's arrived.*" but, of course, he did no such thing.

Though he did not dismiss or seem to doubt any of what I had told him, he seemed unfazed and I cannot begin to express how comforting that was. He said something along the order of really not knowing why I was given this consolation. We talked some more. He prayed for me, and we prayed together. He was able to normalize all of this for me—all of this which was exceedingly *not* normal. My feeling of being somehow anointed vanished. The relief, the relief. *The relief.*

I can now say that his reaction was exactly what I needed at the time. God had chosen Fr. Paul specifically for this task, and had perhaps even inspired him to react in the way that he did. I must say, though, that given what I now know about mysticism, and about the nature and intensity of my experiences, his reaction, both then and since, was curious.

Before we parted, he did give me a warning about the potential for evil or conflict (building on what I had told him regarding my sensing, very directly, evil about, and around me), mentioning St. Catherine's mattress catching on fire, and her various trials. We sat for a moment, just looking at each other. He didn't suggest that we schedule a follow-up meeting, but left it to my discretion. Forty minutes or so after we began, I walked out of his office and into what seemed like a brand new day.

I drove home to my wife and kids. I was still elevated, still very much feeling His physical presence in those points at my shoulders, in the points of light in my chest and stomach, but I was more grounded, in a way. The euphoria that had lifted me to that state of intense elevation had mostly subsided.

My wife made me lunch. I was ravenous. I gave her more details about my experiences that morning. I told her about my meeting with Fr. Paul. I told her that I thought it was now "over." My earnest thought was that God had bestowed these several days of intense grace on me for reasons only He knew, and that the whole experience was now over. I was relieved, so relieved.

Through a nervous yet comforting withdrawal I went to the Y with my family that afternoon. I sat off to the side, my mind never far from the events of these past five days, while I watched them joyously swim.

Day Six

Monday, November 7, 2011

I woke up feeling more myself, but still depleted and groggy. Though wary, I looked forward to the day. My kids would be back at school from the weekend, and I could return to *Virtue*. But more than anything I was looking forward to a resumption of my life as I knew it.

From the moment the Holy Spirit had come to me six days prior I had been completely immersed in my experience. My entire mind, my entire *being* had been consumed—at times by ecstasy, at times by fear, at times by wonder, at times by questioning, at times by great joy. I was exhausted. I was forever changed for the better, and I knew I had much to think about, and pray about, and to live for; but, as I awoke that morning, I simply wanted to be *me* again.

Despite what I had repeatedly professed to my wife over those first few days—*I'm still me*—I wasn't, I hadn't been; or, perhaps it is better said that I had been, in a way, a truer me, a more elemental me, one who was more aware of His existence, more overtly conscious of the beauty and goodness inherent in His world, and, importantly, more aware of the world's brokenness. I had been living, in a way, more profusely, more directly, through my soul. I had been given a heightened awareness of the spiritual realm, not just in the way of direct contact with the Holy Trinity, but in being given a very direct understanding of the *very real* spiritual state that we are all a part of, that we all exist in, that encompasses all of us in *this* world. It was amazing, all of this, these ecstasies, these interactions; my ability to sense evil about me, around me; that I recognized His real presence in the Eucharist; that all that was around me—people, nature, man's creations—possessed such meaning and importance and depth. All of this is, in fact, *true*, but we are all so skeptical of that which we cannot *directly* see. My initial reaction of, *My God, it's all true!* related not just to scripture itself, but to all that could be derived by a theological embrace of scripture, all that we are taught or can be taught, should we give ourselves over to learning more about the very essence of our existence. Again, incredible.

But I will say yet again that living in this state of persistent elevation, a state that is not part of our ordinary human experience was so incredibly *taxing*. I had been given this most blessed grace, this truest and best gift a person could ever be given—*I had experienced Truth: God, Himself!*—but it was all so much for me to handle. Given my own weakness in simply being human, and being as impure as I was, I just wanted it to end. And given the events of the previous day, with all of the drama of the morning, with the rapturous experience of blessed and ethereal detachment, and with the seeming crescendo that had been my meeting with Fr. Paul, I fully expected to be back to my pre-experience state. However, it was, again, not to be.

Soon after waking, after a brief early morning downstairs, I went to my office with the idea that I would work for a short while before bringing my twins to school. But just as I was about to sit down to write, the points of light entered into my chest and stomach, those two prominent points inside each shoulder, and the "holy crackling" began to erupt. But most disconcertingly, I began to experience that ascendant elevation, that hyper-awareness, that *floating*. This was incredibly deflating, and distressing. It is apt to say that I felt, again, in a state of *crisis*.

I was angry. I did not want this anymore. *Leave me alone!* I urged Him. Why was this still happening to me? Why was it continuing? Was this to be my state for the rest of my life? What more did He want from me? What did He have in mind? *What did He want me to do?* Fr. Paul's words about the potential for some manner of demonic attack were still with me —indeed, I hadn't even needed his words on that day to know that it was possible; I had known this was a possibility from the very moment, on Day Two, that I had been given the sense of evil in the world, and of evil around me. And it had been from that very moment, that moment at the playground on Day Two, that I had really, truly, wanted the experience to end. And here I was, days later, with so much having happened in between, and still *experiencing*.

I paced about my bedroom and office, experiencing an oncoming and increasing elevation that was not unpleasant, but which was simply building on top of my utter depletion. If I wasn't quite "anointed," something was still going on and the prospect of what my outcome might be was overwhelming. I went downstairs.

In conversation with my wife I was vague in terms of how I was feeling. I had made a resolution to attempt to *ignore* what was going on, hoping that, somehow, then it would go away. In no way was I *rejecting* what was happening to me. I recognized that in doing so I would be rejecting God, but I just wanted it to *stop*. In attempting to gain some control, I simply resolved to try and be the *me* that I had known for the forty-three years up to that point.

I drove my twins out to their school, elevated and floating and lightly euphoric, experiencing, though less intensely, all of those sensations from the previous morning when I had been so nearly *out of body*. I was anxious and nearly frantic. I didn't know where to turn. I thought of my parents. I hadn't heard from them over the weekend, which was deflating. I couldn't understand, in light of everything I had told them—*I was having mystical experiences!*—that they wouldn't even check in to see how I was, or what was happening. Did they doubt? Did they just not want to hear it? Was it just too strange? I decided to call them after dropping off the twins. At the very least they needed to know all that had happened since I had last spoken to them on Friday, and this would give me a measure of comfort.

I called my father from the parking lot outside my children's school. I brought him up to date, through tears and emotion. As I drove, the pins and points pulsing greatly, the warmth and euphoria very present. Being able to talk to my father was of great comfort to me, and he was supportive, both amazed by my continued experiences and comforted in knowing that I had spoken with a priest. I told him I was still experiencing this grace and didn't know when this would end. I told him that I needed him and my mother, and that I needed to be able to speak to them about this. He—of course—agreed.

I arrived home resolved to simply carry on. I went to my office and began to read *Virtue* from the beginning, lightly editing, and simply working to bring the prose in that first section (of four) in line, stylistically, with the rest of the piece. As I worked I was still in the midst of great elevation, and while not quite euphoric, I did feel satisfied and warm and loved. And I was encouraged by what I was reading. I thought it was good, and this was a relief. As any writer can attest, one rarely has complete confidence in even a finished work. And as I have said, at least in my own mind, and at least as it related to those people who knew what I was experiencing, the piece had a lot to live up to.

By late morning I was ready to stop for the day, feeling the elevation heightening, and an associated disappointment. This increased elevation was of a mixed nature. While the euphoria was most definitely present, I was also unsettled, feeling the presence of evil once again, but somehow *more directly*. As I have mentioned, an awareness of evil was very much a part of my experience. The prospect of evil coming to me in some way or in some form was never far from my mind. It contributed to my exhaustion. I was aware of every noise, every movement around me. I didn't like being alone, particularly at night. In the evenings before all this transpired I would read in my office or engage some solitary task, but now my children all of a sudden found me watching kids' shows with them while waiting for everyone to go to bed—*together*. For me, it was reminiscent of a particular phase in childhood when, after having seen *The Exorcist*, I would crawl into bed with my little brother after he had fallen asleep simply in order not be alone. And believe me, that movie and the knowledge that demonic possession, or even attack, *is real*, was never far from my mind throughout these days.

Part of my disappointment that morning related to a specific awareness of potential interaction with evil that had been growing in me. As my experience during those eight days continued, the more certain I was that some type of interaction might occur. It was difficult to bear. And at that time, in the late morning of day six of my experiences, I was feeling that presence more and an almost inevitable possibility for an encounter. I was well aware of Padre Pio having brawled with the devil, of other saints and mystics being either attacked or approached, and in so many different ways. I couldn't bear it any more. If something was going to happen, I wanted to know. *I wanted to know.* I paced about the house, and then decided to take a walk. I had a destination in mind.

I headed toward the Western Promenade, which is at the western edge of my neighborhood, and took a short five minute walk. The Promenade is at the top of a promontory; a physical, elevated edge to the west side of the peninsula that makes up Portland's in-town area. From the Prom, one can see the valley below extending for dozens of miles, and well into the next state, all the way to the white mountains of New Hampshire. On a clear day Mt. Washington is easily visible. If something, some type of encounter was going to take place, I wanted to know it, and I wanted it to happen now, and I wanted it to happen in the daylight. I didn't think I had much control over the matter, but I simply needed to act. I chose that spot having in mind Jesus being tempted by the devil in Matthew 4. In Matthew 4 the devil brings Jesus to a point of elevation in the mountains, to look out on the world, promising Him all that He can see if He will just bow down. While my heading to the promontory may seem grandiose, I had no delusions that I would be faced with such a situation and I certainly, in wondering whether I was "anointed," did not consider myself a savior. But the increased tension I was feeling, the increased awareness of evil begged some type of action. What I was feeling was very real (and would be validated the next day,) and I simply didn't know what else to do.

The day was warm for that time of year, and sunny. I had expected that there would be people on the

Prom. Maine Medical Center is close by, and workers from the hospital and people from the neighborhood are often sitting on the benches, or walking or running on the path that runs the length of the Prom. As I approached from the northeast, I saw that there were a scattering of people about. This was comforting. When I was perhaps fifty yards from the edge of the promontory, I noticed, approaching from the east, a man who was yelling and shouting and loudly talking to himself. He was clearly either schizophrenic or, I was thinking then, possessed. Had I continued on we would have arrived at the same spot at the same time, right at the edge of the Prom. *No*, I thought, my nerves giving way. *I am not doing this.* I stopped and turned right, avoiding any direct meeting and potential conflict. Amazingly, right then my eyes were drawn to a bumper sticker on a parked car. It read, "Fueled by Faith, Not by Fear." Clearly not a coincidence. All of this was so surreal. And though I was still unsettled, a sense of assurance came over me. I returned home, still very elevated though in a more peaceful state of grace. I couldn't, of course, rid myself of the image of that man, and what some interaction might have been like.

Compounding this unease, that afternoon, that evening, and early the next morning, I was given a number of overt signs that portended a direct interaction with evil that I care not to share in the context of this book. It was that next morning, Day Seven, when my fear would be realized.

Day Seven

Tuesday, November 8, 2011

I woke that morning again feeling elevated and depleted. The points were at my shoulders, the "holy crackling" was present in my chest and stomach. I lay in bed for a while, wondering what the day would bring. Before long, my twins came in. My wife usually takes responsibility for the kids when they first wake up, but she was still asleep so I brought my twins downstairs.

I made coffee and then sat down on the couch with them and turned on a children's show. I picked up my *Magnificat* and on the first page I turned was an intense, ghastly and emotional painting of a crucifixion by Caravaggio. It was unsettling. It clearly wasn't Christ, and I wondered who this was. I read the description. It was St. Andrew. It pierced me. *St. Andrew?* I couldn't help but feel, *What does this portend? Andrew?* I sat there, afraid and discouraged, elevated and yet so depleted. At the same time, I was oddly, resolute. Though I never stopped wondering when this whole experience would end, I had at least resigned myself to keep going, to manage whatever I could, and to hope and pray for God's continued guidance. This may seem like an odd, or even obvious thought, asking for God's guidance, given that He was so clearly with me, that He so clearly "knew" what was going on. He was, after all and in fact, the author of it. But I knew that He was giving me these experiences, and as I had said to my mother and to my wife, this could only be good. I knew it and I believed it. But something being "good" does not necessarily equate with its being "easy." It was clear that I was being tested throughout this great grace, and that I would emerge from it even stronger. I knew this implicitly, and I want to be clear that I leaned, tremendously, on Him during these days. I was reluctant to reach out to Him at times simply because I wanted this to end, and whenever I prayed, or whenever something good and holy was occurring around me, my soul's feeling of closeness increased, and this increased my elevation; again, it was this elevation that was making my bodily existence, both mentally and physically, so very challenging. As I have said, a purer person, a holier person, a person who had developed a closer and more intimate relationship with God may have indulged the experience more than I did, let himself be more immersed, more carried away in trust; I don't know. I did the best that I could during that magnificent trial. I really did.

In any event, when it was time, I brought my twins out to their school. After I got back in the car and began to drive, a wave of intense nausea and extreme disorientation came over me—or I should say, was attempting to *overtake* me. I recognized right away that this was not *normal*—and that this was not God. Nausea is not an apt descriptor of what I felt. It is perhaps better described as a sort of pernicious sickness, and the disorientation was clearly due, from the moment it emerged, to an attack. *"NO!"* I shouted, repeatedly, steeling myself. I fumbled for the lever that controlled the window, seeking air, feeling something working against me, while I continued to shout.

"NO!"

"NO!"

I gripped and gritted, fighting for control, it seemed, of *my very self.* I kept driving, shouting, feeling that stopping would be a form of capitulation and that I couldn't allow that to happen. I struggled. I fought, simply, more than anything, by *willing* whatever it was to depart.

"NO!" I continued to say, resolved to not let this happen. This was not going to happen to me. This was not going to happen to *ME!*

With His protection, it didn't. The attack lasted approximately thirty seconds. It departed in the same way it arrived: quickly. When it was over, I simply continued driving, back to my house, exhausted and dumbfounded. Given all that I had been experiencing, I just carried on. Again, what else was I to do? The attack itself was not at all what I might have expected, and I didn't dwell on it. In any case, despite my exhaustion I was resolute. I cannot say that I had any great sense that something similar would not happen again, but I most definitely felt stronger and less afraid of the prospect.

When I got home I didn't mention the incident to my wife. I was intent upon ignoring it. Even bringing it up, I felt, might bring on another attack. And furthermore, I was very self-conscious, and was still feeling a light sense of shame—this was all so incredible, so emphatically unusual and otherworldly. I had gone from a simple being with an ordinary human experience to a being experiencing something quite different—and I alone was experiencing it. I so needed my wife to be supportive, and part of me wanted her to be reassured that I was, as I had been telling her, still *me*. Being attacked by the devil or a demon—this was not exactly a characteristic of the guy she met in a bar and fell in love with.

As I look back at it, it's rather incredible, but I simply went about my morning. I edited *Virtue* for style, had lunch, went and picked up my kids and proceeded on into the night, feeling all the while elevated and affirmed, anxious and loved, amazed and thankful, and still, lightly, afraid; but most of all *blessed*. I felt the blazing grace of His presence inside me. Interestingly, and perhaps unsurprisingly, I went to bed that night feeling that the end of my experience was near.

Day Eight

In terms of dramatic events, this day was relatively free of them. I woke up still elevated and still feeling, off and on, the points of light, the two points inside my shoulders, and the "holy crackling." All of what I was feeling, though, was less intense than at any time over the previous three or four days. I dropped my children off at school. I worked on *Virtue*, and did regular afternoon and evening things with my family.

The next day, for the first time since the Holy Spirit had entered me so forcefully eight days prior, I began to feel like *me* again.

But that me, of course, would never be the same.

Epilogue

I began sending out *Virtue* to prospective publishers in January, 2012. I made no mention of my experiences over those eight days—it hadn't even occurred to me to do so. Then, and for many months thereafter, I began to simply try to understand all that had happened to me. Of course, I will never fully grasp this in this lifetime.

But in my attempt to at least *better* understand what had happened to me, those first months were filled with prayer, study and reflection. Though surrounded by people who loved me, and feeling, always, loved by God, I was still very much alone in all this. I ordered and read many books on mysticism—books written by mystics, books about them, and about the phenomena—attempting, at least, to put my experiences in context. These books helped, but they were purely, as books are, informational.

My wife and I had on-going conversations. She has been with me every step of the way; and I with her. For several months, though, I told no one else of my experiences. I simply knew I wasn't ready, that it wasn't time. I did not get back in touch with Fr. Paul, and I spoke, only occasionally, to my parents.

As I sought greater understanding, God continued to bestow many graces upon me. And I continued to have mystical experiences. I am not compelled, now, to divulge all that has happened to me since those eight

89

days ended, but I can say that as I continue to grow in my conversion, my experiences have changed and grown as well. What I can say, though, is that the sustained elevation that I experienced over those eight days has not returned. I now recognize that elevation as a special gift, a special grace. Though thoroughly disorienting and trying, that elevation availed me the experience of living—in a very real way—between worlds. It availed me the experience to live, at times frighteningly, through my imperfect soul. And through that experience I was exposed to a further truth of our human existence. We are truly, as it is said, "in the world, but not of the world." Because this is true, there are so many implications, but only one that really matters, and from which life itself flows. To this end, I will simply repeat that first cogent thought I had on that very first day: "It's all true!" My goodness, the implications.

+++

In late February, I finally decided to reach out to someone about my experiences. Interestingly, perhaps, I reached out not to an official member of the church for pastoral care or guidance, but to an expert on mysticism, an academic. I explained very briefly, in an e-mail, some of what I had experienced. My hope was that his response would be along the lines of, "Oh, I hear from one person a week about this..." But that was not his response. His response was short and vague and polite, and I understand this now as appropriate. If I had experienced what I said I had, I was in God's hands, not his. In reaching out to the academic I was still seeking to normalize my experiences—to normalize *myself.* The question continued to surface: *I'm still me, right?* While I recognized that the answer was an emphatic *Yes,* as I have said more than once, I was, of course, forever changed—and forever changing, as we all are. Through His continuing grace, I was growing in my ability to pray, in my willingness to go to Him, to trust. But I was still unsettled. I had experienced God in a way so few people ever do, yet I was still living, very much, in the world and in the context of everything about the world that was still *truly* the same.

To say I struggled—*struggle*—with this would not be inaccurate. Though I was fundamentally, elementally the same me, I had been given this *most blessed* knowledge, this *most blessed* awareness. Yet there I was, walking the streets of my neighborhood greeting neighbors, walking the halls of my children's school greeting teachers and fellow parents, walking the aisles of the Cathedral, greeting friends as that same someone who is ostensibly known—but yet so *unknown.*

None of us is fully understood, of course. No one knows all there is to know about each one of us, except God, Himself. But what I had experienced, what I had been made to know, was and is so categorically *important.* No, I was not, in fact, still *me!* Or at least not *that* me. I had experienced God, was *still* experiencing God, in an extraordinary way. I don't know why He chose me for this. But there I was, and here I am, making small talk, complaining about the Red Sox, shopping for food with my family, visiting my in-laws, coaching my sons in basketball, watching television, retrieving the mail. All normal things, to be sure, and all part of life for an average American man living in the world. I just happen, also, to have this incredible, experiential knowledge that has put everything—*everything that I in my limited power can grasp*—into perspective.

There can be no more elemental an understanding of who we are as humans than the one I have. None. I write this with tears in my eyes. Why me? One would think I would be so *changed*, and while I am to some degree, I am ashamed to say that I am still a magnificent sinner; vain and foolish and prideful. But I am trying to be better, trying to grow closer, trying to achieve what He wants me—all of us—to do in this life, and that is to *truly* seek Him, to *truly* know Him and to *truly* love Him.

As for *Virtue*, over the course of that spring and early summer the rejections from publishers kept coming in, one by one. Some publishers were good enough to send a personalized response. The responses varied from the perplexed to the laudatory. One publisher asked me "what I was trying to accomplish," another wrote, "*Virtue* is stunning—but we don't publish poetry." Every publisher passed. As a writer, this was depressing. But more importantly, as someone who had experienced God as a result of writing this book, this was *perplexing*. If the book was not going to be published, what *did* He want from me in all this?

At some point early in the summer of 2012—before I had heard back from the last of the publishers—I came to know that *Virtue* was incomplete; not in and of itself, but that there was something meant to go alongside it. It wasn't until just recently, nearly a year later, that He showed me how to do it. And now, this book, containing both *Eight Days* and *Virtue*, is before you.

Finally, I must simply say that my journey to Him continues; and that any journey to Him can only be fully made through Christ, Jesus. I have a long way to go, to be sure, but I am finally learning to relent, at least just a little, and He is showing me the way. Pray for me in this, as I will pray for you. Relenting and trusting Him is what He wants from, and for, all of us. In light of this, that he chose *me* for what I have experienced—and not someone holier, or more worthy —can perhaps, in this context, make good sense.

Humbly, and in Christ, Jesus

Andrew McNabb

May, 2013

VIRTUE

I. Power

Of course there is only one sun. Of course there is only one moon. Of course there is a moon at all, because despite the darkness, God never leaves us. In the darkness of our personal nights, God never leaves us.

Us.

God.

God.

Us.

Of course there is only one sun, as there is one God. Of course there is only one moon, as there is one God. It is his plainest message. I am here. I am here. Just look up, I am here.

Just look up, I am here.

I am here.

Just look up.

At the sun.

The sun.

Just look up.

At the sun.

The moon.

The sun.

The sun.

And that there is one sun, as there is one God. If there were no sun, just as if there were no God, there would be no life.

Life.

If there were no sun, just as if there were no God, there would be no life, but life is, and there is one sun, as there is one God; simply raise your face to feel the brilliance.

The brilliance.

Life.

Life.

Life!

Life is; under the brilliance of the sun.

Life.

Life.

Life!

Under the brilliance.

The brilliance of the sun.

The brilliance of the sun, and we cannot gaze directly into it. We cannot gaze directly into the sun, just as we cannot comprehend the ineffable infinitude of God. We cannot comprehend the ineffable infinitude of God and sun, yet the sun is there for us to contemplate, just as God is there for us to seek to know.

To know.

God is there for us to seek to know, because God is life, and so we cannot know life, truly, without knowing God.

God.

God!

We cannot know life without knowing God.

God.

God!

We cannot know life without knowing God, and what else is there to know but life, and thus God.

God, life.

What else is there?

What else is there to know, but life and God?

What else is there?

God, life.

God.

God.

God.

God.

God!

Life!

God is.

God is life, and we are, but only because He is.

He.

He.

He is.

He is, and we are, but only because He is.

He who is, He who will be.

He.

He who is, He who will be.

He.

He.

He is, and we are, but only because

He is.

He.

He.

He is, and we are, and He will be,
and so should we be, too.

So should we be.

So should we be.

In Him.

In Him, He who is.

He.

He who is.

He.

He.

He who is.

He.

II.

But the sun.

The sun.

Entire lives are spent studying the
sun; its composition, its past, its relation to
the other stars, to the planets, to the rocks

101

on Mars, to the plants on earth, to the oceans, to the animals, to the atmosphere, to ourselves.

Ourselves.

Ourselves, and still, we will never know all there is to know. We cannot touch the sun. We cannot even approach it. But still, we try, and should.

And should.

Still, we try, and should.

And should.

And even then, what of the sky?

The sky.

What of the sky; the blue, the gray, the black of night, flowing on, and into, forever.

Forever.

How is it that the blue, the gray, the black of night flows on, and into, forever?

Forever.

Forever.

Forever!

Forever!

The majesty, this boundlessness.

This boundlessness, into forever.

The majesty, this boundlessness—
but also, the miracle, of the bound.

The bound.
The miracle, of the bound.
The bound.

We, us. The bound. For now. The
bound. And the miracle of all that is bound
right near us; the animals that fly or
otherwise propel, the creatures of the
ground, carapaced, scaled, furred or
feathered, living, living, so often, so often,
wanting for nothing, nothing, absolutely
nothing, nothing, and so should we be,
wanting for nothing, and so should we be,
wanting for nothing, because as it is written,
"Now ask the beasts to teach you, and the
birds of the air to tell you; or the reptiles on
earth to instruct you, and the fish of the sea
to inform you. Which of all these does not
know that the hand of God has done this?
In his hand is the soul of every living thing,
and the life breath of all mankind."[1]

All of this, all of this, all of this
under the great and airy clouds that float.

1 JOB 12:7-10

Float.

The great and airy clouds that float.

Float.

The great and airy clouds that float,
these clouds, these clouds, these majestic,
floating dreams.

These dreams.

These dreams.

These majestic, floating dreams,
some colliding, some combining, some
simply scatting forward untouched on their
way to somewhere else in this ultimate
daytime drama that so often goes unnoticed.

Unnoticed.

Unnoticed.

Unnoticed, this.

Unnoticed, this, but how is it?

How is it?

How is it that the immensity of this
performance can be so overlooked?

How?

How?

The immensity of this performance
can be so overlooked because life is
limitless, His fruits are everywhere, and
within us, His greatest creation, there is a
raging, vibrant complexity that is ever-

seeking, ever-evolving, always new. New.
Ever-evolving, always new.

Us.

We.

We, us.

New.

New.

We, us, new, and this complexity
can be blinding, indeed, in its own light, its
own light that is pure blackness next to
God's, that needs God's light to even flicker.

God's.

God's light.

God's.

God's light.

God's.

God.

God.

God's light.

God's.

God.

God.

God.

III.

And the sun.

The sun.

The earth's fine spin around the
sun, enabling an earthly rhythm, providing
for us, with each dawn, renewal.

Renewal.

The earth's fine spin around the
sun, enabling an earthly rhythm, providing
for us, with each dawn, renewal, so that
each morning we emerge from the cloak of
night transformed; transformed by the
night, though the sun really never stopped
shining. Throughout the darkness we were
never really alone.

Alone.

Throughout the darkness we were
never really alone.

Alone.

Alone, and the sun is, just as God
is, but the sun is not God, though God is
the sun. But what if the sun was not quite
the sun? What if the sun was slightly

different in composition, a fraction closer, a fraction farther away? This multitude of life would not exist.

      Life.

      Life.

      Life!

      This multitude of life would not exist.

      Life.

      Life.

      Life!

      Is it cosmic fluke that one mere planet away not a living thing has ever been known to exist, but that on this great earth every color of the rainbow lives and breathes in countless shapes and innumerable forms? Is it mere happenstance that here on this sphere so many life forms do not merely exist, they rejoice, jumping and playing and buzzing and building and blossoming and creating and pro-creating, animated, simply, by their very existence? What of the odds? What of the essential, intricate interdependence? And what of the singular awe inherent in each of these individual miracles?

What of it?

What of it?

What of it, because must blue tides crest? What of it, because must flowers awaken, explode? What of it, because must trees reach, and rivers run wide, and water be so utterly, thoroughly cleansing? And must, and must, and must a parent's love for a child—the closest experience we have to experiencing God's limitless love for us— be so utterly selfless?

No.

No.

No.

No.

No, of course not; everything could be gray and locked, or everything could be nothing at all, and so it is, just as it is written: God created the world and it was good.[2] God created the world and it was good and God created humans and gave them dominion over the world, and what was good gave way to greatness.

---

2 GN 1:31

Greatness.

Greatness.

Greatness.

What was good gave way to
greatness.

We are great.

Greatness, we are great, because
what is greatness?

Greatness.

What is greatness?

Greatness.

Greatness, at its most absolute, is
indestructability. Indestructability.
Greatness, at its most absolute, is
indestructability. Indestructability. God
has made us indestructible. It is nearly
impossible to fathom the breadth of this,
this eminence we have been granted. Once
conceived, we will exist forever.

Forever.

Once conceived, we will exist
forever; a fate and a power that surpasses
that of any mythical creature, any fairytale
imagining, any modern-day superhero,
because it is real.

109

Real.

And it is truth.

Truth.

It is real, and it is truth, we were conceived, and so we exist. We are temporal body, and everlasting soul. We are in this world, but not of this world. We are alive; we live. We live. We will live.

Live.

Live.

We will live, but what, really, does it mean to live?

To live.

What does it mean to live?

To live.

In this present life, to live is to think, to feel, to act, to be.

To be.

In this present life, to live is to think, to feel, to act, to be, and to live is to have free-will, free-will, and thus to live is to make decisions. Our lives are a continuum of decision-making, existing as we do from moment to moment, every moment fresh.

Decisions are life.

Life is choices.

This, too, is greatness: we choose.

We choose.

We choose.

No one chooses for us, we choose, and in choosing we have been given direction. In choosing we have been given His Natural Law, and we have been given the Word.

The Word.

We have been given the Word.

The Word.

We have been given the Word, and, "In the beginning was the Word, and the Word was with God, and the Word was God."[3]

God.

God.

We have been given God, Himself.

We have been given God, Himself, and what more could there be? What more could there possibly be?

But God.

What more could there possibly be?

---

3 JN 1:1

And what more could we possibly have
been given, but God?

    God.

    But God.

    God.

    What more could we possibly have
been given, but God?

    God.

    God.

    God.

    And we are told that, "God,
infinitely perfect and blessed in Himself, in
a plan of sheer goodness freely created man
to make him share in His own blessed life.
For this reason, at every time and in every
place, God draws close to man. He calls
man to seek Him, to know Him, to love
Him with all his strength."[4]

    To seek Him, to know Him, to love
Him.

    To seek Him, to know Him, to love
Him.

    That is it.

    That is it.

---

4 *Catechism of the Catholic Church*, 1.

We are to seek Him, to know Him, to love Him, with all our strength. This is our purpose. This is our purpose in life. Our purpose. We are to seek Him, to know Him, to love Him.

That is it.

That is it.

But how?

How are we to seek Him? And how are we to know Him? And how are we to love Him? In short, how are we to live?

Live.

How are we to live?

Live.

In Ecclesiastes, it is written: "Let us all hear together the conclusion of all matters: Fear God, and keep his commandments."[5]

The conclusion of all matters.

The conclusion.

The conclusion of all matters.

The conclusion.

That is it.

That is it.

---

5 Ecclesiastes 12:13

Fear God.

And keep His commandments.

This is how we seek Him, how we know Him, and how we love Him.

By fearing Him.

And by keeping His commandments.

By fearing God.

And by keeping His commandments.

Fear God: acknowledge His supremacy, submit to His will.

Fear God: acknowledge His supremacy, submit to His will.

His will.

His will.

His will: Keep His commandments.

His will: Keep His commandments.

His commandments.

His commandments, because in keeping His commandments we have nowhere to go but to love itself, to Him.

To love itself, to Him.

Love.

Love.

114

In keeping His commandments, we have nowhere to go but to love itself.

Love.

Love.

We love in fearing God, and in keeping His Commandments.

That is it.

That is it.

Fearing God, and keeping His Commandments.

That is it.

That is it.

That is it.

And thus all of the seeming complexity of this life has been reduced to, and is to be processed through, the Commandments handed down first to Moses by God,[6] and then simplified and perfected by God's own Son, our Lord and savior, Jesus Christ.

To Moses:

I.   I am the Lord, your God, You Shall Not Have False Gods Before Me

---

6 EX 20:2-17

II.   Do not take the name of
your Lord, God, in vain

III.   Keep Holy the Sabbath

IV.   Honor thy father and thy
mother

V.   Do not kill

VI.   Do not commit adultery

VII.   Do not steal

VIII.   Do not bear false witness
against your neighbor

IX.   Do not covet thy neighbor's
wife

X.   Do not covet thy neighbor's
goods

We are reminded by Pope Benedict
XVI that these Ten Commandments "are
only an explanation of love's ways; we read
them correctly only if we read them in Jesus
Christ."[7]

Jesus Christ.

Jesus Christ.

We read these commandments
correctly only if we read them in Jesus

7 *Catechism of the Catholic Church*, "Introduction," Joseph Cardinal Ratzinger.

Christ, who, knowing our limitations, but also our potential, infinitely expanded our responsibility, even while simplifying these ten into two:[8]

From Jesus:

I.   "You shall love the Lord, your God with all your heart, with all your soul, and with all your mind."

II.   "You shall love your neighbor as yourself."

He said, "The whole law and the prophets depend on these two commandments."[9]

Love the Lord. Love your neighbor.

On these two commandments depend the whole law.

Love the Lord. Love your neighbor.

On these two commandments depend everything.

Everything.

Everything.

Everything.

8 MK 12:29-31

9 MT 22:37-40

On these two commandments
depend everything; but what is everything?

Everything.

What is everything?

Everything.

Everything, is the only thing.

Everything, is the only thing, that
matters.

Matters.

Everything, is the only thing, that
matters.

Matters.

Everything, is the only thing, that
matters, and the only thing, that matters, is
our relationship with God.

Everything, is the only thing, and
the only thing, that matters, is our
relationship with God—and to God.

And to God.

And to God.

And to God, because we are to
become like Him, we are to become love.[10]

We are to become like Him, we are
to become love, but only through Him, and

10 1 JN 3:2

with Him, because apart from Him we can do nothing.[11]

Nothing.

Apart from Him, we can do nothing, we are nothing.

Nothing.

Apart from Him, we can do nothing, we are nothing; but we are to be everything.

Everything.

We are to be everything, because everything is the only thing.

Everything, is the only thing, and everything, is Him.

He is everything.

He is everything, and we are to become like Him, but only through Him.

We are to become like Him, but only through Him, and with Him, and in Him.

We are to become everything.

We are to become everything, like Him.

We are to become everything, too.

---

11 1 JN 15:5

Too.

Too.

We are to become
everything, too.

IV.

We are to become everything, too,
because if we do not become everything, we
become nothing.

Nothing.

If we do not become everything, we
become nothing.

Nothing.

And what is nothing?

Nothing.

What is nothing?

Nothing, is the absence of Him.

Nothing, is the absence of Him.

There can be nothing less than this,
because He is everything.

Everything.

There can be nothing less than this,

because he is everything, and if we do not
have Him, we have nothing.

Nothing.

We have been told.

We have been told.

We have been told, and it is at this
that St. Augustine said, "The Gospel
terrifies me."

For it is in the Gospel that we are
reminded of the four last things: Death.
Judgment. Heaven. Hell. We are destined,
each, for three.

Death.

Judgment.

Heaven.

Hell.

We are destined, each, for three.

Thomas Á Kempis wrote, "Well for
you if you keep an eye on your deathbed all
the time." In Ecclesiastes 7:40, it is written,
"In all thy works, remember thy last end,
and thou shalt never sin." And Á Kempis
again, with the perspective of a man who
has lived life right: "Strange that you should
look forward so little to the Day of

121

Judgment," for after all, is St. Augustine not perfectly correct in his lament, "[Lord,] our hearts are restless until they rest in you."

In you.

In you.

"[Lord,] our hearts are restless until they rest in you."

In you; and in scripture, we are reminded, time and again, of our responsibilities in this earthly life.

It has been written. And we have been reminded. We have been told. We have been told.

We have been told.

We have been told.

It has been written. And we have been reminded. We have been told.

Told.

We have been told.

Told.

We have been urged, time and again, to love God, and to love each other.

We have been urged, time and again, to love God, and to love each other, with all our heart, all our soul, and all our might, not simply because of a looming judgment, but because this love is the only means to peace, both in this life, and in the next.

In this life, and in the next.

This love is the only means to peace, both in this life, and in the next.

In this life, and in the next.

In the next.

In the next.

In the next, because it is as we have been told, "Lo, the day is coming, blazing like an oven."[12] And it is as we have been cautioned, "Two men will be out in the field; one will be taken, one will be left."[13] And it is as we have been promised, that if the love of God is perfected in us, "we will ascend in glory,"[14] and if it is not, we "shall not enter into the kingdom of heaven."[15]

The kingdom of heaven.

The kingdom of heaven.

Because it is just as it has been

---

12 Malachi 3:20

13 MT 20:40

14 Need it

15 MT 5:20

123

written, "I have set before you life and
death, the blessing and the curse; choose
life!"[16]

> Life!
> Life!
> Life!
> Choose life!
> Life!
> Life!
> Life!

> Choose *life!*

V.

Life.
Life!
We are to choose *life!*
But why is it, so often, we do not?
Why is it, so often, we do not?
We ignore, willfully, the splendor of
His word.

We succumb, eagerly, to the
enticements of this world.

We seek, constantly, emancipation

16 DT 30:19

from His will.

We persist, manically, in our
failings.

We persist, manically, in our
failings.

Our hubris brings us only
emptiness and confusion.

Confusion.

Confusion.

Oh, to not understand!

To not understand!

To not understand, is to have a false
understanding, or no understanding at all; it
is to be less than whole. Without
understanding there can be no hope, true
hope, and "The one who has hope lives
differently."[17]

Without understanding there can be
no hope, true hope, and "The one who has
hope lives differently."

We are called to live differently.

Differently.

We are called to live differently.

Differently.

---

17 Pope Benedict, *Spe Salvi*.

We are called to live differently, yet we persist in our failing.

We persist in our failing, but He is patient, He waits.

We persist in our indifference, yet He never leaves us, *He waits!*

We persist in our insult, but he is slow to anger and rich in mercy, and He is quick to forgive.

Forgive.

Forgive.

He is quick to forgive, enduring our shame, while calling to us constantly, constantly, through the big, through the small, through the flush of grace to be experienced in the extraordinary, through the obvious goodness of the every day.

The every day.

The every day.

He calls to us through the obvious goodness of the every day. Beginning with the light.

The light.

His light.

His light.

He calls to us every day through the light, His light. Through the light in the sky in its multi-hue, through the light in the sky where light is not just light, but countless shades that we can name or not name, because color ascends to infinity the way that numbers do, the way that space does—the way that we do.

The way that we do.

The color in the light ascends to infinity, the way that we do.

The way that we do.

We, us!

We, His greatest miracle.

We, His greatest miracle.

St. Augustine said, "Men go forth to wonder at the heights of mountains, the huge waves of the sea, the broad flow of the rivers, the extent of the ocean, and the courses of the stars, and they omit to wonder at themselves."[18]

Themselves.

Ourselves.

Wondering at ourselves is

---

18 Augustine, *Confessions.*

wondering at God and this is good and
pleasing to Him because true exploration
can only lead us toward Him, because we
are of Him, we are from Him, in His image.

His image.

We are of Him, and we are from
Him, in His image.

His image.

We, us.

This, us.

This, all of us.

This, this hand!

This, this hand, this mighty hand!

This hand, this hand, this mighty
hand!

Raise it through the air!

Adjust the fingers slightly, or
greatly, or lightly, in unison, or individually,
together, apart, by virtue of some unseen
power emanating from the brain, the
mind...and maybe even the soul.

Thought, thought!

Thought!

Thought!

The power of thought, so abstract—

where, in fact, is it?—yet so concrete, so measurable, at times, at least, physically, mentally, even spiritually.

Spiritually.

Spiritually.

The power of thought.

The power of thought.

Thought.

Thought.

The power of thought, so measurable, at times, at least, physically, mentally, even spiritually.

Spiritually.

Spiritually.

Thought.

Prayer.

Awareness.

Our awareness that we are.

We are...

He is...

We are...

He is...

...but this hand!

This hand.

This hand.

This hand, this most intricate,
expressive, self-healing tool, all tendons, and
bone, and nerves, and blood, responding to
thought, contained by this skin, this skin,
this inimitable skin, its imprint unique to us
in this most clear expression of our
individuality in God's eyes, in this most
profound announcement that it can be no
other way.

No other way.
It can be no other way!
Way.
It can be no other way!
Way.

This hand, this hand, attached to
the rest of us, no less overwhelming; our
durable softness, our intense uprightness,
the peculiar beauty of our features, our
limbs.

Our limbs.
The peculiar beauty of our features,
our limbs.

Our features.
Our features.
Because what of beauty's function,

and what of beauty's depth?

The eye!

To see!

Sight!

We look!

Why?

Why?

Why should we—or any of God's creatures—*see?* How could it be just some natural evolutionary end? Why should something without an eye develop one? Why should something without an eye develop one, this bodily component so perfect in itself, so complex, so complex— and so meaningful.

Meaningful.

So meaningful.

How is it that a bodily part can have such transcendent function?

Function.

How is it that a bodily part can have such transcendent function, can be so much more than a means for physical perception?

Perception.

131

How is it that this eye, in all its functional glory, is so much more than a means for physical perception?

The beauty.

The power.

The glory.

The beauty of a shade, the power of a glance, the glory of what a glance can render, the intelligent power of that subtle glance, its endless possibilities.

Possibilities.

Its endless possibilities.

Possibilities.

And function's beauty, that window to function's depth.

The eye!

Sight!

To see.

To see.

To *see!*

The infinite allure of an eye's shade, striking no matter the hue, its constellation of skittered streaks, its centers' bottomless depth, escalating, constricting, adjusting, intensifying, converging, converging,

converging on life's next wonder. The
meaning, the meaning, the profundity.

We see!

We *see!*

We see because He wants us to see.
We see because He wants us to witness His
creation; the world, each other, ourselves.

Ourselves.

We see because He wants us to
witness ourselves, and in witnessing
ourselves, Him.

Him.

We see so that we can witness
ourselves, and in witnessing ourselves, Him.

Him.

We see so that we can witness Him.

Him.

Him, and thus ourselves.

Him.

Him.

Him, and thus ourselves.

Him.

Him.

Him.

Him.

VI.

Him.

Because of Him, we are able to see ourselves, truly, but only if we see ourselves, ably.

Ably.

Because of His light, we are able to see ourselves, truly, but only if we see ourselves, ably.

Ably.

If we see ourselves, ably, we see Him, truly.

Truly.

If we are able to see Him, truly, that is it.

It.

That is it.

It.

Seeing Him truly, is it.

It.

Seeing Him truly, is it, because in

seeing Him truly, we see ourselves truly,
and in seeing ourselves truly we recognize
our poverty, and in recognizing our poverty,
we recognize His supremacy, and in
recognizing His supremacy and our poverty,
all is right, all is ordered, all is correct.

Correct.

There is no greater knowledge than
this, no greater wisdom.

There is nothing more.

Than this.

This.

This.

There is nothing more.

Than this.

This.

This.

Because this is everything.

Everything.

This.

Is everything.

Everything.

This, is everything.

Everything.

Everything.

This.

This.

This, is everything, but our poverty, is anything, but poor. Our poverty, is blessed. Our poverty, is blessed, because our poverty, seeks. Our poverty, seeks, because our poverty, aches.

Aches.

Our poverty, aches, and thus we seek, a salve.

A salve.

Our poverty, aches, and thus we seek, a salve.

A salve.

In aching, we act, seeking, a salve.

A salve.

To ache, is to be poor, to be poor, is to be human, to be human, is to ache, and in aching we seek a salve.

A salve.

In aching we seek a salve, and we feel it, this seeking, and we see it, this seeking, and we live it, this seeking, throughout the machinations of our days, driving our relationships, fueling our thought, powering our actions, and this, all this, with all this, determining, our fate.

Our fate.

Our fate.

How we handle the ache of our poverty determines our fate.

Our fate.

How we handle the ache of our poverty determines our fate, because handling the ache of our poverty is life itself.

Life.

Life itself.

Handling the ache of our poverty is life itself, and so life itself is understanding our poverty, and thus understanding His supremacy, and thus acting, in accordance, with each.

Our inclination is to conquer, to vanquish, to elevate.

To elevate.

Our inclination is to conquer, to vanquish, to elevate, but our poverty, this poverty, our poverty, is not destitution, and so we cannot, materially, conquer, and vanquish, and elevate in this way.

Our poverty, is anything, but poor. Our poverty, is us. We are, our poverty. We are, our poverty, and we are, blessed. We are, our poverty, and we are, blessed, and so our poverty, is blessed, and the way, to salvation, is not to conquer, our poverty, because our poverty, is blessed, and it is just as we have been told, "Blessed are the poor in spirit, for theirs is the kingdom of heaven."[19]

Heaven.

Heaven.

"Blessed are the poor in spirit, for theirs is the kingdom of heaven."

Heaven.

God.

Heaven.

"Blessed are the poor in spirit, for theirs is the kingdom of heaven."

Blessed are the poor. Blessed is our poverty. To be poor, in this way, is to be blessed. To recognize, our poverty, is to be blessed. In recognizing, our poverty, we

---

19 MT 5:3

accept, life's clouds.

Life's clouds, life's useful clouds.

In recognizing, our poverty, we accept, life's clouds. Life's clouds are obligatory, life's clouds are mandatory, life's clouds will always be; because what blue sky will never see clouds again? What blue sky will never see clouds again? Life's clouds are pain, and life's clouds are suffering, and life's clouds will always be. Life's clouds will always be, but life's clouds are not our ache.

In recognizing our poverty, we recognize that life's clouds are not our ache.

Our ache is our separation from Him, emanating from Original Sin. Our ache is our separation from Him, emanating from Original Sin. It has made us poor. Original Sin has made us poor, has deprived us of the only riches that are everlasting, the riches that are Him, that are union with Him.

With Him, that are union with Him.

With Him, that are union with Him.

Life's clouds are there to remind us,
that there is no salve but Him.

But Him.

Life's clouds are there to remind us,
that there is no salve but Him.

But Him.

But it is due, to our poverty, that we
often fail to recognize, our poverty,
properly, and it is due, to our poverty, that
we seek to solve life's clouds, improperly,
treating them as our ache.

Our ache.

It is due, to our poverty, that we
attempt to conquer life's clouds, to vanquish
life's clouds, to elevate beyond them, while
our feet are still firmly planted; but life's
clouds are not our ache.

Our ache.

Life's clouds are not our ache.

Life's clouds are not our ache,
because even under a clear blue sky, we
long.

We long.

Even under a clear blue sky, we
long.

We long.

Even under a clear blue sky, we long.

We long.

Even under a clear blue sky, we long, because life's clouds are not our ache.

Our ache, is our absence, from Him.

And so our only salve, is union, with Him.

With Him.

Our only salve, is union, with Him.

Our only salve, is union, with Him, and life's clouds are there to remind us, of Him, of life, of life's true sun. Life's clouds are there to remind us, and the brightness of that blue sky sun is there, as a promise.

A promise.

That blue sky sun is there, as a promise.

A promise.

The sun, our salve.

That blue sky sun is there, as a promise, and with this promise, there is hope.

Hope.

With this promise, there is the only true hope.

Hope.

With this promise, there is the only true hope, and with true hope, though life's clouds may be, life's hope outlasts all.

Life's hope outlasts all.

And though life's clouds may be, they are useful in remembering Him, and His promise. We lament the duration of our trials, but "If God puts off answering us," said St. John Chrysostom, "it is solely to keep us near Him for a longer time."[20] And as Evagrius said, "God delays in giving us what we need, perhaps first of all, because He enjoys hearing us speak to Him."[21]

Him. Our salve.

Him. Our promise.

Him. The only cure to our ache.

Our ache.

Our ache.

Him, the only cure to our ache.

20 *Magnificat*, May 21, 2011. "Meditation of the Day," Fr. Bernard Bro, O.P.
21 *Magnificat*, May 21, 2011, "Meditation of the Day," Fr. Bernard Bro, O.P.

Our ache.

Our ache.

Him, the only cure to our
ache.

VII.

Our ache.

Our ache, can be cured, under this
sun.

It can.

Our ache, can be cured, under this
sun.

It can.

It can.

Our ache, can be cured, under this
sun, despite life's clouds, and despite the
chasm of life's Original Sin.

Our ache can be cured under this
sun, if we relent, if we relinquish.

It is what He wants, our
relinquishment.

It is what He wants, our

relinquishment, so that love's rays may heal,
so that love's rays may fill and heal, and so
that we, too, can become love.

Love.

Love's rays.

Love's healing rays.

But love's rays heal, only, with our
relinquishment.

Our relinquishment.

Love's rays only heal, with our
relinquishment.

Our relinquishment.

Our relinquishment, and so, how do
we?

How do we?

How do we?

How do we?

How do we relinquish, and thus
handle, the ache, of our poverty, our
poverty?

How do we relinquish?

Relinquish.

How we relinquish is life, life itself.

How we relinquish is life, life itself,
in handling, the ache, of our poverty.

Our poverty.

And so, how do we?

How do we handle the ache of our poverty, how do we relinquish?

How do we relinquish?

How do we relinquish?

How do we relinquish?

To relinquish, is a process.

To relinquish, is a blessed process.

To relinquish, is a process, not of hollowing out, but of filling, of fulfilling, of fulfillment.

Fulfillment.

Relinquishment, true relinquishment, is not a hollowing out, but a fulfillment.

Fulfillment.

But how do we relinquish, so as to fulfill?

How do we relinquish, so as to fulfill?

Fulfill.

How do we relinquish, so as to fulfill?

By fulfilling, His expectations.

We relinquish, and thus fulfill, by fulfilling, His expectations.

His expectations, His expectations.

His expectations are that we know Him, serve Him, and love Him, with all our might.

That is it. This is it.

That is it. This is it.

This is it, to know Him, to serve Him, and to love Him, with all our might. And He has given us the means to do so. He has given us Himself, He has given us this life, He has given us His word, He has given us His only Son, true man, true God, He has given us the wonders and presence of His Holy Spirit, He has given us our holy mother church, He has given us the sacraments, He has given us prayer, He has given us the example of the saints, and He has given us the capacity for virtue.

Virtue.

He has given us the capacity for virtue.

Virtue.

Our virtue, we control.

We control, our virtue.

Our virtue, we control.

We control, our virtue.

Virtue.

Virtue.

Virtue, the means by which we access all these other good things.

Virtue.

Virtue.

Virtue, these seven virtues: Faith, Hope, Love; Justice, Prudence, Temperance, Fortitude. That is it.

That is it.

These seven virtues.

That is it.

This is it.

Virtue.

These seven virtues, given to us.

These seven virtues, given to us so that we may access these others great gifts.

These seven virtues, given to us so that through their employment we may obtain His grace.

His grace.

His grace.

His grace, the answer to our ache.

His grace, the answer to our ache, our ache, our incomparable ache.

Our ache, our ache, our incomparable ache.

He wants to heal our incomparable ache because He loves us. He who is love. He loves us. He who is love. He who is love, has given us Himself, His son, His Holy Spirit, His church, His sacraments, prayer, the saints...and He has given us the capacity for virtue.

Virtue.

Virtue.

He has given us the capacity for virtue so that we may access these other great gifts, and so that we may appeal for His grace.

His grace.

His grace.

Because what else is there, but His saving grace?

What else is there but Him, His grace, our salve?

Him, His grace, our salve.

His grace, His grace, His efficacious grace.

His grace, His grace, the end of all matters.

The end, His grace. The only good end, His grace.

His grace, His grace, our salve.

Our salve, Him, by His grace, and only through His grace, because His grace is Him. Him. His grace is Him.

Him.

His grace is Him, our salve.

We appeal for His grace, and thus our salve, through our virtue.

Our virtue.

We appeal for the only salve to our ache through our virtue.

Virtue.

We appeal for the salve to our ache, our great and only true ache, through our virtue, our virtue, and as Pope Leo XIII reminds us, "that virtue, and virtue alone, wherever found, will be followed by the rewards of everlasting happiness."[22]

---

22 Pope Leo XIII, *Rerum Novarum.*

Everlasting happiness.

Everlasting happiness, the end of all matters, the only good outcome, the only good end, to be achieved by our virtue, and our virtue alone.

Our virtue, and virtue alone, achieved only through Him, and by Him, and from Him, and with Him.

Our virtue, and virtue alone.

Our virtue, and virtue alone.

To be followed by the rewards of everlasting happiness, and thus all of the seeming complexity of this life just flakes away, dropping like the scales from St. Paul's eyes.

Everlasting happiness, our everlasting happiness, through our virtue, and virtue alone, our virtue, and virtue alone.

Our virtue, and virtue alone.

Our virtue.

Our virtue.

Our virtue.

Our virtue.

II. Perfection

I.

And so we are.

And so we will be.

But should we just, *be?*

We can never just, be; because of
who we are.

Who we are, is who we will be.

But who should we, be?

We should be who He wants us to

be.

But who does He want us to be?

Us. He wants us to be, us.

Us, and He wants us to be who He
made us to be.

He made us to be like Him.

Him.

He made us to be like Him.

Him.

Him, and in His image we were created. In His image we were created and we grew and we were born, at every step with the penetrating beauty and drama that is life.

Life.

Life, from the demonstrative act that led to our conception, to the miracle of our formation, to the great spectacle of our growth, to our bursting into the light of life.

Life.

Life.

Life!

Into the light of life we burst and were given breath.

Breath, life.

This taking in, this release.

We breathed, we breathe.

We are alive, we live.

We are alive, we live, and in living, in having been created, we have been given a purpose, and in being given a purpose we are compelled to act.

Act.

We are compelled to act.

Act.

We act.

We act, because we are, because we exist, because it is our nature, to act.

In His world we must act so that we may live. If we do not act, we will not live, we will die.

We act, because we are, because we exist.

We are, we exist, in these moments upon moments, every moment fresh, in these moments upon moments, that pass and renew, and so are we, passing and renewing, constantly, in perpetuity, at least in this life, if not for eternity.

It is as He made us.

It is as He made us.

We are, we exist, in these moments upon moments, every new moment bringing new breath, every new moment bringing new life, every new moment bringing new thought, every new moment renewing our need.

Our need.

Every new moment renewing our need.

Our need.

And so we act, because we need, and our actions are powered by our thinking, based in reason, and by our choosing, based in free-will. We think and we choose. We think and we choose. We think so that we may continue to think, and we think so that we may choose and continue to choose.

Because we need.

Him.

We need.

His grace.

We need, Him.

We need, His grace.

But how do we obtain Him? And how do we receive His grace?

The answer is: only through Him, and only from Him, and not from ourselves.

It is only through Him and from Him that we may receive His grace, and we are to take refuge in what He has told us;

"My grace is sufficient for thee."[23]

And He reminds us, "I am the vine and you are the branches...Apart from me you can do nothing."[24]

And it is written, "For by grace you are saved through faith—and this is not from yourselves, for it is the gift of God."[25]

And so it is; but is that it? And so it is, but is that the end of all matters? And so it is, and so should we do nothing but wait for His grace and then elevate?

Certainly not!

We are not simple and impish, relegated to passivity, awaiting His glance and nod. We are vibrant and vital and capable, and He has given us a purpose—*to know Him, to serve Him, to love Him*—and a means to pursue that purpose.

Virtue.

The means to pursue that purpose is virtue.

Virtue.

Virtue.

---

23 2 COR 12:9
24 JN 15:5
25 EPH 2:8

The means to pursue that purpose is virtue.

Virtue, enabling us to pursue life's purpose.

Virtue, enabling us to appeal to Him.

To Him, because we need Him.

He is what we need.

Him.

We need, Him.

Him.

We need, Him.

And we pursue Him through our virtue.

Virtue. This fount within us.

Virtue. This grand empowerment.

Virtue. This most generous gift.

Virtue. This means to an end.

Virtue. Faith, Hope and Love.

Virtue. Justice, Prudence, Temperance and Fortitude.

Virtue. These seven virtues. Three to be used in raising ourselves to God, and in bringing Him down to us. Four to be used in our living in the world, enabling us

to remain steadfast and strong and
righteous in our living and in our
relationships with others.

Virtue.

Virtue.

Virtue.

He has given us the capacity for
virtue.

And "virtue," as Aristotle said, "is
excellence at being human."

And "virtue," as St. Augustine said,
"is that whereby we live rightly."[26]

And "virtue," as St. Thomas
Aquinas said, "is the habit of a happy
heart."[27] A happy heart is peace, and peace
is only possible through knowledge of Him,
through receipt of His grace, and so
knowledge of Him is only possible through
virtue. We can only achieve peace through
virtue.

Virtue. Faith, Hope and Love.[28]

Virtue. Justice, Prudence,

26 St. Augustine, *On Free Will.*

27 Christopher Kaczor, *Thomas Aquinas on Faith, Hope & Love.*

28 1 COR 13:13

Temperance and Fortitude.[29]

Virtue. These seven virtues. That is it.

Virtue. Love. Love is a virtue. "The greatest of these."[30]

Virtue. Hope. Hope is a virtue. And "In hope we are saved."[31]

Virtue. Faith. Faith is a virtue. And "Faith is the substance of things hoped for, evidence of things not seen."[32]

Virtue. Prudence. Prudence is a virtue. Prudence is "the *auriga virtutum*, "the charioteer of all the virtues," guiding all others."[33]

Virtue. Temperance. Temperance is a virtue. "[Temperance], training us to renounce...worldly passions, and to live self-controlled, upright, and godly lives."[34]

Virtue. Justice. Justice is a virtue. "Justice, a joy to the righteous, a terror to the evil."[35]

29 WIS 8:7

30 1 COR 13:13

31 ROM 8:24

32 HEB 11:1

33 *Catechism of the Catholic Church*, 1806.

34 TITUS 2:12

35 PROV 21:15

Virtue. Fortitude. Fortitude is a virtue. "Fortitude strengthens man's mind against that greatest danger, death."[36]

Virtue. These seven virtues. These seven virtues from which all others flow.

Virtue.

Virtue, enabling us to appeal for Him, for His grace.

For Him, for His grace, because we are, and we will be.

Be.

For Him, for His grace, because we are, because we will be.

Be.

Because we are, because we will be.

Be.

II.

We are, and we will be. Just as He is, and He will be. But He was, and we were not. He was, and we were not. But

---

36 St. Thomas Aquinas, *Summa*, II-II.

we are, and we will be, but only because, He
is.

He.

He is.

He.

He is.

And that there is a He.

He.

That there is a He, and He is not
us.

We are only us, because He is.

He.

He is.

He is, and from Him, we are.

From Him, we have come, and to
Him, should we return.

To Him should we return, because
should we not return to Him, to where
should we go?

To where should we go, should we
not return to Him?

To where?

To where; because forever will we
be, and we will always be, somewhere.

We.

We.

We will always be, somewhere, but for now, we are here, and for now, who should we be? Who should we be?

Who should we be?

Who should we *be?*

Who should we be, and in being who we should be, should we be any less than all of who we should be? Should we be any less than all of who we should be, who He intended us to be, who He wants us to be? Should we be half, or three-quarters of who we should be? Or should we be all of who we should be?

We should be all of who we should be.

But who should we be?

We should be who He wants us to be.

And who does He want us to be?

Us.

Us, as He made us.

He wants us to be us, as He made us.

Us, like Him.

He wants us to be like Him. He wants us to be like Him, because we are from Him, created in His image. We have been created in His image, but what is His image?

His image is pure goodness.

His image is pure love.

His image is perfection.

Perfection.

His image is perfection.

Perfection.

His image is perfection, because He is perfection.

Perfection.

He is perfection, and in His image and likeness we were created and so we, too, are to be perfection.

Perfection.

We, too, are to be perfection.

Perfection.

For, after all, what is the alternative?
Imperfection.

Imperfection.

Imperfection.

Imperfection is contortion, a

contorting away from perfection. The
greater the contortion, the greater the
imperfection. The greater the imperfection,
the more hideous we become. Should we be
hideous in His sight? No, "We should be
holy and unspotted in His sight."[37]

Holy, unspotted.

Holy, unspotted.

Perfect.

Perfect.

We should be holy and unspotted in
His sight.

We should be perfect in His sight.

Perfect.

We should be perfect in His sight,
because we are to be like Him, and He is
holy and unspotted.

He is holy and unspotted, and we
should be holy and unspotted in His sight.

We should be like Him; because
what else is there to be?

We should be like Him; because
what more is there to be?

He is perfect, and so should we be

---

37 EPH 1:4

perfect.

He is perfect, and so should we be perfect.

Perfect.

Perfect.

He is perfect, and so should we be perfect. It is what He wants. It is what He expects.

Jesus said, "Be you therefore perfect, as also your heavenly Father is perfect."[38]

Perfect.

"Be you therefore perfect, as also your heavenly Father is perfect."

Perfect.

And so should we be anything less than perfect? No. We should be perfect.

Perfect.

We should be perfect.

Perfect.

Jesus was human, and Jesus was perfect, and so are we human, and thus so can we be perfect.

Perfect.

We do not allow ourselves to think

---

38 MT 5:48

this way. We do not allow ourselves to think that it is possible. This is simply evidence of the imperfection in our lives, of our clinging to the temporal, of our not understanding Him, of our not understanding ourselves, and who we are, and who we can be, and who we will be, and the purpose for which we were created, and above all, this is evidence of our failing to remember our mission in life: to know Him, to serve Him, and to love Him, with all our might.

That is it.

That is it.

This first.

This first.

This first, with all our might, and from this will come perfection.

Perfection.

With all our might.

With all our might.

With all our might—and thus with His grace—perfection, is, indeed, possible.

Possible.

Perfection, is, indeed, possible.

Possible.

Possible.

And because it is possible, it is also possible that it will not be.

Because it is possible, it is also possible that it will not be.

The choice is ours.

Ours.

It can be our choice that we can be, in this life, who He wants us to be.

Who He wants us to be.

Who He wants us to be, but any deviation from our mission is a contortion, and will result in our imperfection. The greater the contortion, the greater the imperfection. The greater the imperfection, the farther away we are from Him, the farther away we are from His love.

His love.

The farther away we are from His love, the less happy we become, and the less fulfilled we will be. And so, by turn, the closer we are to His love, the happier we become, and the more fulfilled we will be.

We will be.

166

The closer we are to Him, and to His love, the closer we are to the end for which we were created. The closer we are to Him, and to His love, the closer we are to perfection.

Perfection.

The closer we are to Him, and to His love, the closer we are to perfection.

Perfection.

Perfection, the end for which we were created.

Perfection.

Perfection, the end for which we were created.

Perfection.

What else is there, but perfection?

Perfection.

What else is there, but to be perfectly aligned with His will?

His will.

His will.

What else is there, but to be perfectly aligned with His will—He who is, He who was, He who will be.

He.

He.

Because He is.

He is.

Because He is, and He is who He says He is.

He is.

He is.

He is, and He is who He says He is.

He is.

He is.

He is, and He is who he says He is, and so are we who He says we are, and so are we to be who He says we are to be.

To be.

To be.

We are to be who He says we are to be.

To be.

To be.

We are to be who He says we are to be, because if we are not who He says we are to be, we are less than what we should be.

If we are not who he says we are to be, we are less than what we should be, and

why should we be anything less than what
we should be?

Why?

Why?

Why should we be anything less
than what we should be?

Why?

Why?

Why should we be anything less
than what we should be?

And what should we be? Who
should we be? Who does He want us to be?

Us.

He wants us to be us, as He made
us.

He wants us to be us, as He made
us, in His image.

Us.

He made us, in His image, and His
image, is perfection.

Perfection.

He made us, in His image, and His
image, is perfection, and so are we to be
perfection.

Perfection.

We.

Us.

We.

We.

We who are, we who will be, but
only because He is.

He is.

We who are, we who will be, but
only because He is.

He is.

He is, and we are, and so will we be.

We are.

We are, and so will we be.

We are, temporal body. We are,
everlasting soul. We are temporal body,
and everlasting soul.

Soul.

Soul.

Everlasting soul.

Soul.

Soul.

Everlasting soul.

Soul.

Soul.

Soul.

We are, everlasting
soul.

III.

"O beauteous soul!" wrote St. Francis de Sales, "Since you can know God why do you beguile yourself with lesser things?"[39]

Indeed, why?

Why?

"Since you can know God, why do you beguile yourself with lesser things?"; through the body, through the spirit, through the whims and whimsy and afflictions of the body, through the pollution of the spirit, the spirit, the very essence of we, the spirit. The spirit, so influenced by body, the temporal body, and the spirit, so influencing the body, the temporal body.

The body, the temporal body.

The body, the temporal body, beauty and responsibility, beauty and

---

39 St. Francis de Sales, *Introduction to the Devout Life*, 5:10.

responsibility, because as St. Paul wrote, "Know you not that [your body is] the temple of God and that the spirit dwelleth in you?"[40]

Dwelleth in you; dwelleth in us.

Us.

Us!

The spirit dwelleth in us.

Us!

Us.

The spirit dwelleth in us.

Us.

Us!

The spirit, His spirit, is perfection.

Perfection.

The spirit, His spirit, is perfection, and the spirit dwelleth in us. The spirit is perfection, and the spirit dwelleth in us, as much or as little as we let it. As much or as little as we let it, and it should be much, it should be much, indeed, it must be much.

Much.

Much.

Indeed, it must be much, and we

40 1 COR 3:16

have been instructed to "cleanse ourselves
from every defilement of flesh and spirit,
making holiness perfect in the fear of God."[41]

Perfect.

Perfect.

"Making holiness perfect in the fear
of God."

Holiness. Perfect.

Perfect. Holiness.

Perfection.

We are called, this way, to
perfection.

Perfection.

We are called, this way, to
perfection, by cleansing ourselves from
every defilement of the flesh and spirit.

By cleansing ourselves.

By cleansing ourselves, in this life,
in this day.

In this life, in this day, as our
primary vocation, and not as some spiritual
supplement to our earthly lives.

In this life, in this day, as our
primary vocation, and not as some spiritual

41 2 COR 7:1

supplement to our earthly lives.

Our earthly lives.

Our earthly lives.

Our spiritual vocation is our
primary vocation, now. Our spiritual
vocation is our primary vocation, now,
because it is just as we have been instructed,
"It is the hour now for you to awake from
sleep. For our salvation is nearer now than
when we first believed; the night is
advanced, the day is at hand. Let us then
throw off the works of darkness and put on
the armor of light."

Light.

Light.

Let us put on the armor of light.

Light.

Light.

"The day is at hand;" yet still, we
contort.

We contort.

"The day is at hand;" yet still, we
contort.

We contort.

We contort away from Him. We

contort away from perfection.

We contort away from Him. We contort away from His love.

We contort away from Him, disfiguring ourselves into an approximation of wholeness we perceive to be right, or, at least, "Good Enough."

"Good Enough."

"Good Enough."

How good, is "Good Enough?"

How good, is "Good Enough," and when we arrive there, how will we know?

How will we know, how good, is "Good Enough?", and how will we know when we arrive there.

How good is "Good Enough?"

"Good Enough."

"Good Enough."

How will we know, how good, is "Good Enough?"

How will we know, how good, is "Good Enough," when "Good" is an amorphous, subjective, ever-changing standard?

How will we know how good is

"Good Enough" when "Good" is an amorphous, subjective, ever-changing societal standard?

How?

How?

How will we know, how good, is "Good Enough?"

"Good Enough."

"Good Enough."

How?

How?

How will we know, how good, is "Good Enough?"

The answer is, the answer can only be: We will not know. We cannot know. We will not know, because we cannot know. We cannot know, because this is not taught, because this is not Truth.

How good is "Good Enough," is not taught, because it is not Truth, part of Truth.

It is not Truth, part of Truth.

How good is "Good Enough," is not Truth, part of Truth, and thus it is not taught, it is not taught.

But what is taught, is the one alternative.

What is taught, is perfection's pursuit.

What is taught, is to never stop growing toward Him, toward His light, toward His love, toward His love, in pursuit of a perfect union with Him, in pursuit of perfection.

Perfection.

Perfection.

What is taught, is to never stop growing toward Him, toward His light, toward His love, toward His love, in pursuit of a perfect union with Him, in pursuit of perfection, perfection, perfection, because in pursuit of this, there is redemption, and in pursuit of this, there is perfection, itself.

Perfection, itself.

In pursuit of perfection, there is perfection, itself, because as St. Gregory of Nyssa reminds us, "This is truly perfection: never to stop growing towards what is better and never placing any limit on perfection."[42]

Perfection.

Never to stop growing towards what is better, and never placing any limit on perfection, for this is truly perfection.

Perfection.

Perfection.

In this pursuit of perfection, there is perfect knowledge. In pursuit of perfection, there is perfect knowledge because there is perfect acknowledgement, of Him, and thus perfect acknowledgement, of ourselves.

Of Him, of ourselves.

Of Him, of ourselves.

Of Him, of ourselves.

IV.

When we acknowledge Him, as supreme, and ourselves, as impoverished, there is perfect knowledge, and perfect

42 St. Gregory of Nyssa, "Meditation of the Day," *Magnificat*, 4/5/11.

acknowledgment, and in this perfect knowledge, and in this perfect acknowledgment, our path is perfectly clear.

Clear.

In this perfect knowledge, and in this perfect acknowledgment, our path is perfectly clear.

Clear.

Our path is perfectly clear, and though we have been given a choice, we have no choice. Though we have been given a choice, we have no choice, but to follow Him, as He instructs us. In our perfect acknowledgment of Him, we have no choice, but to love. We have no choice, but to love Him with all our strength, with all our might, with all our strength, with all our might, with all our strength, with all our might, with all our strength, with all our might, and to love each other, as ourselves, and to love each other, as ourselves, and to love each other, as ourselves. In this pursuit, there is perfection.

Perfection.

In this pursuit, there is perfection, and we are not to misunderstand this pursuit, this most necessary and worthwhile pursuit, as being outside of our reach. We are not to misunderstand this pursuit of perfection as something that cannot be achieved, because what kind and merciful and all-knowing father would ask for what he knows cannot be achieved? Our God does not expect from us what we cannot achieve, what we cannot achieve.

Achieve.

Our God does not expect from us what we cannot achieve.

Achieve.

Our God does not expect from us what we cannot achieve, each of us. Our God does not expect from us what we cannot achieve, each of us, and we have been so ably reminded of this, recently, in that great document heralding the light of life at the dawn of the third millennium, *Novo Milenio Inuente*. In this great document we have been reminded, we have been reassured:

"This ideal of perfection must not be misunderstood as if it involved some kind of extraordinary existence, possible only for a few "uncommon heroes" of holiness. The ways of holiness are many, according to the vocation of each individual...The time has come to re-propose wholeheartedly to everyone this *high standard of ordinary Christian living:* the whole life of the Christian community and of Christian families must lead in this direction."[43]

The ways of holiness are many; but holiness, it is.

The ways of holiness are many; but holiness, it must be.

The ways of holiness are many; and we are all called to the perfection of holiness in our lives, to the perfection of holiness as the requisite standard of *ordinary* Christian living, of *ordinary* Christian living.

We are all called to the perfection of holiness, as a matter of course, as a matter of life itself. We are all called to the

43 Pope John Paul II, *Apostolic Letter Novo Milenio Inuente.*

perfection of holiness as the requisite standard of *ordinary* Christian living, of *ordinary* Christian living.

We are all called to the heroism of holiness.

Holiness.

We are all, no matter our vocation, called to the heroism of holiness.

We are all, no matter our vocation, called to the heroism of holiness, and holiness, true holiness, is perfection.

Perfection.

True holiness is perfection.

Perfection.

True holiness is perfection, and we are all called to holiness, and thus we are all called to perfection, as the standard of our *ordinary* Christian living, our *ordinary* Christian living.

We are all called to perfection as the standard of our *ordinary* Christian living, because our ordinariness is us, we are our ordinariness.

We, us.

Our ordinariness is us.

We, us.

And so this call to holiness, to perfection, is made with regard to our own particular circumstance, because it is through this circumstance that life is lived.

Lived.

It is through our own particular circumstance that life is lived, and each of us, no matter our circumstance, lives life through the smallness of one moment giving way to the next. Life is lived through the smallness of one moment giving way to the next, and it is in these small moments that we are faced with life's small challenges. And this is life.

Life.

And this is life.

Life.

And this is life, not one grand challenge to be overcome, conquered, but a series of small challenges faced in small moments, small challenges faced in small moments, with small upon small upon small adding up to the bigness of a life, to the bigness of accumulated moments that makes us us.

Us.

That makes us us.

Us.

Small upon small upon small adding up to the bigness of accumulated moments that makes us us, and so we are to be heroes of the small.

Small.

We are to be heroes of the small.

Small.

We are to be heroes of the small, and thus heroes of the everyday. We are to be heroes of our thoughts, and heroes of our actions. We are to be heroes of our actions, and heroes of our interactions. We are to be heroes, of simple acts.

Simple acts.

We are to be heroes, of simple acts.

Simple acts.

We are to be heroes of the small.

We are to be heroes of the everyday.

We are to be heroes of the small, heroes of the small.

The small is life, as it is lived. The small is us, every day. The small is us,

every day, in our decisions, in our decisions;
in our deciding to open up, or to be closed
off; in our deciding to engage, or to look
away; in our deciding to say yes in simple
matters of love and righteousness, or to say
no; in our deciding to sympathize, to feel, to
take on another's sorrow, another's
challenge, another's vulnerability, or to
simply live unto ourselves. In the smallness
of our lives, in the smallness of our lives'
moments, we are often deciding whether to
place another's needs before our own.

> Our own.
>
> Before our own.
>
> Our own.
>
> Before our own.
>
> Our own.
>
> > Before our own.

V.

In our smallness, we are often
deciding whether to place another's needs
before our own, and this is the essence of
practical living, of practicality, and
practicality is the essence of smallness.

Smallness.

Practicality is the essence of smallness, and it is our performance in small moments that add up to the bigness of a life. It is our performance in small moments that reveals our practicality, and our attention to smallness.

Smallness.

Practicality is attention to smallness, and we are to be heroes of practicality, and thus heroes of smallness, heroes of smallness.

Smallness.

We are to be heroes of attention to smallness, and thus heroes of our practical lives as we live them. In being heroes of smallness, we are heroes of humility, because humility is acknowledgement of the smallness of ourselves.

Ourselves.

Humility is acknowledgement of the smallness of ourselves.

Ourselves.

Humility is acknowledgement of the smallness of ourselves, and of the bigness of our Creator, and in this acknowledgment, in this understanding, in this wisdom, is the acknowledgement of the immensity of our own worth. In acknowledging—and in living—His will, through our love and humility, we acknowledge our relationship to God, and with God, and in this we acknowledge His boundless love for us, and thus the immensity of our own worth.

Our own worth.

The immensity of our own worth.

Our own worth.

In acknowledging His great love for us, we acknowledge the immensity of our own worth, and thus the immensity of our own destiny. In acknowledging the immensity of our own destiny, we acknowledge our obligation to be heroes of ourselves.

Ourselves.

We fulfill our obligation to be heroes of ourselves, by being heroes of our smallness, by focusing on what St. Therese called "The Little Way."

"The Little Way."

"The Little Way."

"The Little Way," is the way of smallness.

Smallness.

"The Little Way," is the way of smallness, and life as it is lived, is the way of smallness. Life as it is lived is lived moment upon moment, small moment upon small moment, and so life as it is lived should be life lived according to "The Little Way," "The Little Way."

"The Little Way," is perfection and excellence in daily small acts, perfection and excellence in the way of smallness.

Smallness.

"The Little Way," is the way of perfection.

Perfection.

"The Little Way," is the way of perfection.

Perfection.

"The Little Way," is the way of smallness, of smallness, of excellence in smallness.

Smallness.
Smallness, our life.

Smallness.

Smallness, our life, this life, this compilation of small acts, of small act upon small act, small act upon small act. Smallness, our life, this life, this accumulation, of smallness, that adds up, to the bigness, of a life.

Life.

This accumulation, of smallness, that adds up, to the bigness, of a life, true life.

Life, true life.

Life, this accumulation, of small moments, this compilation, of small acts, small acts, and we are called to be heroes of this smallness, heroes of this small vision. We are called to be heroes of this small vision, because in this accumulation of small moments is the largest vision imaginable. This largest vision imaginable is Jesus Christ, Himself.

Jesus Christ, Himself.

Jesus Christ...

...

Himself.

Jesus Christ, Himself, who could
have ruled the world as a triumphant king,
but who was a simple carpenter, who was a
simple carpenter, attending to the smallest
things.

Jesus Christ, Himself.
Jesus Christ...

...

Himself.

Jesus Christ, Himself, who loved,
who sacrificed, who knew no bottom to
humility. If we see this largest vision of
smallness, of the perfection to be wrought
in smallness, we understand the greatness of
smallness, we understand the greatness that
can be ourselves, in our smallness.

Our smallness.

We understand the greatness, of our
smallness, in our attempt, at perfection, in
our small ways, in our small, every day,
ways.

Perfection.

Perfection.

We understand the greatness, of our
smallness, in our attempt, at perfection, in

our small ways.

Our small ways.

And He helps us.

He guides us.

He helps us.

If we let Him.

If we let Him.

He guides us.

He helps us.

He has given us Himself, He has given us this life, He has given us His word, He has given us His only Son, true man, true God, He has given us the wonders and presence of His Holy Spirit, He has given us our holy mother church, He has given us the sacraments, He has given us prayer, He has given us the example of the saints, and He has given us the capacity for virtue.

Virtue.

He has given us the capacity for virtue so that we may access all these good things, and access them perfectly.

Perfectly.

Perfectly.

Perfectly, through our virtue.

Virtue.

Perfectly, through our virtue.

Virtue.

Perfectly through, our virtue.

He has given us the capacity for virtue so that we may access all these good things through our virtue.

Virtue.

We attempt perfection in our small ways through our virtue.

Virtue.

Virtue.

Virtue.

We attempt perfection in our small ways through our virtue, which we control, through Him.

Virtue.

Our virtue, we control, through Him.

Through Him, we control, our virtue.

Our virtue.

Our virtue.

Virtue.

Virtue.

Virtue, the means by which we access all these other good things.

Virtue.

Virtue.

Virtue, the means by which we perfect the smallness in our lives.

Virtue, these seven virtues: Faith, Hope, Love; Justice, Prudence, Temperance, Fortitude. That is it.

That is it.

These seven virtues.

That is it.

This is it.

Virtue.

These seven virtues, given to us.

These seven virtues, given to us so that we may access these others great gifts.

These seven virtues, given to us so that through their employment we may obtain His grace.

His grace.

His grace.

His grace, the answer to our ache.

His grace, the answer to our ache, our ache, our incomparable ache.

Our ache, our ache, our incomparable ache.

He loves us. He who is love. He loves us. He has given us Himself, His son, His Holy Spirit, His church, His sacraments, His Holy Mother, the saints, prayer, and He has given us the capacity for virtue.

Virtue.

Virtue.

He has given us the capacity for virtue so that we may access these other great gifts, and so that we may appeal for His grace.

His grace.

His grace.

Because what else is there, but His grace?

What else is there but Him, His grace, our salve?

Him, His grace, our salve.

His grace, His grace, His efficacious grace.

His grace, His grace, the end of all matters.

The end, His grace. The only good
end, His grace.

His grace, His grace, our salve.

Our salve, Him, by His grace,
because His grace is Him. Him. His grace
is Him.

Him.

His grace is Him, our salve.

We appeal for His grace through
our virtue.

Our virtue.

We appeal for the only salve to our
ache through our virtue.

Our virtue.

Our virtue.

We appeal for the only salve to our
ache through our virtue.

Our virtue.

Through our virtue.

Our virtue.

Virtue.

Our virtue.

Through our virtue.

III.   Ensnared

I.

Ensnared!

That there is such a word, so melodious, so profound.

Ensnared.

In a language there could be just one word for anything caught, and that word could be nothing more than pure conveyance; but not on this earth, where language is deep, and life is deeper.

Ensnared.

But why must this word, or any word, have depth? It is a question of life, really. Language only has depth because life has depth. Life has depth because life is possibility; the ultimate possibility. Life is the ultimate possibility because we are not just chance evolutionary outcrop.

Life, is *Life!*

The ultimate possibility.

Life is, indeed, the ultimate possibility, and thus the ultimate opportunity, but opportunity seized is not a certainty. Opportunity seized is not a certainty because we, in living our lives, can become, ensnared.

Ensnared.

We in living our lives, can become, ensnared.

Ensnared.

Ensnared.

That a word can be so full, can mean so much, can have such depth—and that if a mere word can have such depth, how much depth have we?

We.

If a word can have such depth, how much depth have we; we, this very essence of depth, if by depth, and according to that most straightforward definition, we mean distance.

Distance.

We are the very essence of depth,
because once created, we are eternal, and
there is no greater distance than distance in
time.

Time.

Once created, we are imperishable,
everlasting, and there is no greater distance
than distance in time, yet our depth exceeds
even this definition because now created, we
will not just exist forever, we will exist in a
state of grace, or in a state of disgrace.

We, us.

Forever.

Grace, or disgrace.

We, us.

Forever.

This is Truth, because it has been
written.

Truth.

This is Truth, because it has been
written, that we are from Him, in His
image.

Truth. Truth, itself.

This is Truth, because we are from
Him, in His image, He who was, He who is,

He who will be.

Be.

He who was, is and will be; and so now are we, in His image, and thus so will we be.

Be.

We.

Depth.

There can be no greater depth, and so it is in this, in this endless depth, that there is the ultimate responsibility. There is the ultimate responsibility because it is we ourselves who determine the direction of our depth—toward life, or toward death.

Death.

Life.

Life.

Death.

It is strictly true, and it can be no other way, for it is just as it is written, "I have set before you life and death, choose life!"[44]

Life.

Choose life.

44 DT 30:19

Life!

The enormity of this responsibility!
Life!

For if life is a choice, then death is a choice, too. If life is a choice, then death is a choice, and the enormity of this responsibility is made explicit by our very depth.

Depth.

The enormity of this responsibility is made explicit by our very depth, by our very importance, by our very significance, because such matters are not left to the shallow, to the unimportant, to the insignificant.

We are deep, and we are important, and we are significant, and in this, the responsibility of choosing life over death has been given to us.

Us.

We.

This responsibility, so grave.

But we are not alone in this, not left to ourselves. He is with us.

Us.

He is with us in this.

This.

If we choose. But the choice is ours.   And in choosing, how could it be that a person could choose death over life?

Life.

How could it be that a person could choose death over life?

Life.

It could only be that if in choosing death, a person believes he is choosing life. But how could it be that a person choosing death believes he is choosing life? It could only be in the lusty confusion of worldly and bodily entanglement, this most treacherous ensnarement, choking reason and smothering truth.

Truth.

Life.

There is only life, true life, in Truth.

Life.

In Truth.

There is only life, true life, in Truth, and so there is only something less than life, true life, in the absence of Truth, or in the perversion of Truth.

Truth.

The perversion of Truth is death's most proud accomplishment. Death becomes life in the perversion of Truth, this most insidious and evil and pernicious ensnarement, because it is most common.

Common.

Common, most common.

The perversion of Truth is death's most proud accomplishment, because it is most common.

Common.

Common, most common.

Because it is not necessarily that in Truth's perversion that right is wrong, that up is down, that death is life; it is that what is truly wrong is not believed to be wholly wrong, and that what is truly right is not believed to be wholly right. Elements of truth may remain, giving an appearance of truth. An appearance of truth gives comfort to those seeking an answer from which the difficult has been extracted. Over time this perverted truth becomes the accepted truth, for many.

Many.

Over time this perverted truth becomes the accepted truth, for many, and so it is in this perversion that there is the greatest danger, with even the well-intentioned making wrong choices believing they are right. It is in this perversion that even the well-intentioned— *"the good"*— become ensnared.

Ensnared.

Ensnared.

It is in this perversion of Truth that even "the good" become ensnared, and in becoming ensnared, even "the good" risk losing true life.

Life.

True life.

In becoming ensnared, even "the good" risk losing life, true life. And becoming ensnared is a possibility because we don't just exist, we live. In living we have been given reason. In living we have been given free-will. And so in living we think, and in living we choose. It is by this, by our thinking and by our choosing, that we are truly human, that we are truly alive.

We live.

It is by this, by our thinking and by our choosing, that we are truly human, and thus truly alive.

We live.

It is by this that we are truly human, by this that we are truly alive, by this that our lives are animated, and by this, and according to this, that we will be judged. It is by this, by our choices, that we will be judged.

Judged.

It is due to the nature of our choices —good or bad—that we can even be judged at all. It is due to the very presence of goodness, and badness, that we can even be judged at all, because if all choices before us were good, there would be no such thing as opportunity with regard to possibility. Life would just be.

Be.

And if all choices before us were bad, there would be no such thing as opportunity with regard to possibility. Life would just be.

      Be.

      Be.

      Be.

                  Life would just, be.

II.

But there is good, and there is bad, and there cannot be good without bad, and there cannot be bad without good. And thus there is good, and thus there is bad, and so life does have depth, and life does have meaning, and so life is possibility, the ultimate possibility, and thus the ultimate opportunity.

      Opportunity.

      Opportunity.

But opportunity seized is not a certainty, because we, in living, can become ensnared.

      Ensnared.

Ensnared, but how?

Ensnared, by what?

Ensnared.

Ensnared by the body, ensnared by
the mind.

Ensnared.

Ensnared by ourselves, ensnared by
others, ensnared by what we, together,
create.

Ensnared.

Ensnared by the needs of the body.

The body.

Ensnared by the desires of the body.

The body.

But what is the body?

The body is this vessel, this most
blessed vessel. The body is this most
wondrous creation, this most beautiful
assemblage. The body is this life. The body
is this. This body. This. This flesh. This
physical extension of our soul. This carnal
object, infused with life. His life.

Life.

His life.

Life!

Breath, life. Given. Granted. In His glory, if we let it be. If only we would let it be. If only we would just, let it, be.

Be.

Be.

We don't often just, let it, be. Our body, for us, becomes us, becomes all.

All.

But all, in this way, is not everything. Only life—true life—is all. True life, is all, and true life, extends. True life, extends, beyond the us of our bodies, beyond the us of ourselves.

Ourselves.

True life extends beyond the us of ourselves, but it is this physical us, this most obvious us, this us before our eyes, this most apparent us, that is, too often, prevailing. Too often, this bodily us, prevails.

Prevails, and ensnares.

Too often, this bodily us, prevails, and in this, we are, we become, ensnared.

Ensnared.

In this, we are, we become,

ensnared. Ensnared by the body, ensnared.

Ensnared.

Ensnared by the needs of the body.

Ensnared.

By the body.

By the body.

This body.

This body, this crying need. This body, this present must. This body, this fleshly extension, this fleshly contraction. This body, this spot, this moving spot, this smallness, this largeness, this occasion, this ever-present occasion. This body, this present means.

This body, this present means.

This body, this present means, seeking an end, an end, an end; but by the body alone, the end is different than by body and spirit.

Spirit.

By the body alone, the end is different than by body and spirit.

Spirit.

We are body and spirit, and spirit and body are life, true life, and life is more than food and the body more than clothing, and though "the spirit may be willing, the flesh is weak."[45]

The flesh is weak.

Through the insistence of the flesh we can become ensnared.

Ensnared.

Through the insistence of the flesh we can become ensnared.

Ensnared.

The flesh, the flesh.

The flesh, this flesh, this flesh that can be seen. The flesh that feels, that can be felt. The flesh this goodness, this supreme goodness, because it is from Him, of Him, He who is goodness, pure goodness.

Goodness, pure goodness.

This flesh can only be goodness, because He, Himself, "became flesh, and dwelt among us."[46] If He became flesh, and He is goodness, then this flesh can only be goodness, pure goodness.

Goodness, pure goodness.

---

45 MK 14:38

46 JN 1:14

If He became flesh, and He is goodness, then this flesh can only be goodness, but we are not He, and He is not us, and we, in this flesh, can become corrupted.

Corrupted.

We, in this flesh, can become corrupted.

Corrupted.

Ensnared.

We, in this flesh, can become corrupted by things that appeal, only, to the flesh.

The flesh.

We, in this flesh, can become corrupted by things that appeal, only, to the flesh, and the things that appeal, only, to the flesh, are the things that the eye can see.

See.

The things that appeal, only, to the flesh, are the things that the eye can see; but can the eye now see God? No. The eye cannot see God, and so the flesh is not concerned with God, the flesh is only concerned with that which it can see, that which it can touch; but can the flesh now touch God? No. The flesh cannot touch God, and so the flesh is not concerned with God, the flesh is only concerned with that which it can touch.

See, touch.

Touch, see.

The eye cannot see God, the flesh cannot touch God, but the mind—that which, itself, cannot be seen—can contemplate God. The mind can contemplate God, and thus the mind can know God, in conjunction with the spirit.

God.

God.

God!

In knowing God, true life is known.

Known.

Known.

In knowing God, true life is, known.

III.

In knowing God, true life is known,
but in knowing God, we do not necessarily
know God, truly, because our mind can be
corrupted, just as our flesh can; and our
flesh can be corrupted, because the mind
can be corrupted, because the flesh does not
act independently of the mind. So the mind
is of the flesh, and the flesh is of the mind.
If the flesh can be unconcerned with God, it
is only because the mind can be
unconcerned with God. Though the mind
—entwined with the flesh, and entwined
with the spirit—can know God, it does not
necessarily know God, truly.

Truly.

The mind does not necessarily know
God, truly.

Truly.

The mind does not necessarily know
God, truly, because though the mind is

entwined with the spirit, it is also entwined with the flesh. The flesh has no concern for God, because the flesh cannot know God. The flesh responds only to that which it can see, to that which it can touch.

Touch.

Though God can be seen in all good things, the flesh desires the primal, physical satisfaction it can derive from the world.

The world.

The flesh desires only the primal, physical satisfaction it can derive from the world. In this there is danger; because not all is pure base. The desires of the flesh are not all pure base, because the mind can incorporate experience to elevate us, spiritually and intellectually, enabling the whole of us to *'see'* God in the beauty of the world, and *'touch'* God in his physical creation.

See, touch.

Sensation.

Sensation.

The sensation; the sight, the feel. And how much of life, how much of the world is sight, and feel; sensation?

Sensation.

Sensation.

How much of life, how much of the world, is sensation? Much, very much; and it is in this, in this reality, that the sensational, base desires of the flesh can overwhelm, because the objects of these desires are right before us in the world.

The world.

The objects of our base desires are obvious to us in the world, while the only true satisfaction is less obvious, on the surface, and so it is in this imbalance of sight and feel that there is the greatest danger, if in what we see, and in what we touch, become, in and of themselves, aspirational.

Aspirational.

We, by our very nature, aspire.

Aspire.

We are aspirational, and in fulfilling our aspirations we constantly ask, What shall I see? And what shall I touch?

See, touch.

We move through our days seeing and touching, and thus we are asking and answering the questions—What shall we see? What shall we touch?—from morning to night. We answer by our actions; what we see is what we want to see, and what we touch is what we want to touch. And what we want to see and touch is largely what pleases us. But what is it that pleases us? What is the root of our pleasure? By our very nature, we seek the pleasure of happiness, and in this there is goodness, because it is as we were made, to seek happiness.

Happiness.

But what is it that pleases us, what is it that makes us happy? Is it purely that which we can see, that which we can touch? How much of what we want to see, and what we want to touch is pure sensation, and how much of what we want to see, and what we want to touch enables our mind to elevate to that good end for which we were created—to know Him, to serve Him and to love Him?

How much?

How much?

How much of what we want to see, and what we want to touch is pure sensation, and how much of what we want to see, and what we want to touch enables our mind to elevate to that good end for which we were created—to know Him, to serve Him and to love Him?

Desire extends beyond pure touch. We are not merely sensual. We see and we feel, but we also think, and interact, and intuit, with each other, and with our world —and with Him.

Him.

We think, and interact, and intuit, with each other, with our world—and with Him, because of Him. With Him, through Him; He who is. With Him, through His creation. With Him, through ourselves.

Ourselves.

It is because of our very depth and complexity that our curiosity is provoked. This curiosity is not limited to exploration of the nature of our existence, of the meaning of our lives. This curiosity, rooted in free-will, can lead us down many different paths, as we seek knowledge and understanding. As we seek experience. In this exploration there is goodness, because it is as He made us.

As He made us.

This world is plentiful. This world is mysterious. This world is inspiring. But in exploration, in seeking to know, and understand, there is also potential danger, potential ensnarement.

Ensnarement.

Ensnarement.

In seeking knowledge, in seeking experience, there is potential ensnarement because in this quest our focus on the world can supplant, or obstruct, our focus on Him.

Him.

Our focus on Him.

Him.

And in this quest for knowledge and experience, there is also an inclination toward conquest.

Conquest.

In our exploration, in our quest for knowledge and experience, there is an inclination toward conquest as an end; but we can never conquer.

Conquer.

We can never conquer the world because we were not created for this end. We were not made to conquer the world, and thus any attempt is failure. If we veer from that end for which we were created, the only result will be loss. If we veer from the true purpose of our lives, our result will only be something less than whole.

Whole.

If we veer from the true purpose of our lives, our result will only be something less than whole, and so just as we ask ourselves—What shall we see? What shall we touch?—we must also ask ourselves: What shall we think about? What shall we focus on?

What shall we think about?
What shall we focus on?
To avoid the snare of self.

Self.

The great snare of self.

Self.

The great snare of self, because, indeed, we can become ensnared by the self, by the desires of the self. We can become ensnared by the self, by the power of the self and, indeed, the self, is powerful.

Powerful.

The self is powerful; it is as He made us.

Powerful.

Our power, in this world.

Our power, over ourselves, in this world.

Our power, in this world; this world that flourishes!

This world that flourishes; the possibility, the possibilities!

Just look about, at all there is!

The abundance, not to be conquered, but to enrich us. The abundance, of the world, not to be conquered, but to enrich us, so that we may fully experience His grace, by this reminder that His grace is everywhere.

Everywhere.

His grace is everywhere.

Everywhere.

His grace is everywhere, in flitting wings, in dropping petals, in the lashes of an eye. His grace is everywhere, in human touch, in water's strength, in the pointed lights of the nighttime sky. His grace is everywhere.

Everywhere.

His grace is everywhere.

Everywhere.

He is everywhere.

His grace is everywhere.

Everywhere.

Everywhere.

Everywhere.

Everywhere.

IV.

He is everywhere, but He is also nowhere, to be seen, at least by human eyes. If He was everywhere, to human eyes, there would be no such thing as free-will, no such thing as a choice to love Him, because God, in His overwhelming light of love, in His radiance of pure goodness, fully exposed to our human eyes, would eliminate any doubt.

Doubt.

He is love. He is love. He is love, true love, and He yearns for our true love in return. But true love is a choice, rooted in true faith. If He holds Himself back fully from our eyes, it is to test our faith, because by faith we erase doubt.

Doubt.

By faith, we erase doubt, and by faith, rooted in Him, we love, true love. By faith, we erase doubt, and by faith, we love, and by our faith, and according to our works, and by the depth of our love will we be judged worthy, or unworthy, of the promises of Christ.

And what else is there?

And what else could there possibly be?

And what else is there, and what

else could there possibly be, but that only good end, that indescribable, ever-present, never-ending joy.

Joy!

That indescribable, ever-present, never-ending joy.

Joy!

And so we are to rejoice, even now. We are to rejoice, even now, in the knowledge of what is to come. We are to rejoice by recognizing Him in what is so plainly there, this abundance.

This abundance, this sensory abundance.

This abundance, this abundance, this intellectual abundance.

This abundance, from Him, to be used in recognition of Him, and to be valued and appreciated only in concert with Him.

Him.

This abundance to be valued and appreciated only in concert with Him, because without Him, we lose focus, and we become ensnared.

223

Ensnared.

Without Him, without recognition of Him in this abundance, we become ensnared.

Ensnared.

We become ensnared because this abundance can overwhelm in its "this-worldliness," in this world in which our bodies compete.

Compete.

We become ensnared because this abundance can overwhelm in its "this-worldliness," in this world in which our bodies compete.

Compete.

This abundance.

This abundance.

This abundance that can be seen, that can be touched, that can be conceived, and thus, because of our weakness, can seduce.

Seduce.

This abundance that can seduce, can become the end, instead of the means because we are so intensely present in these bodies, in these needs, these gaping needs, at least as perceived, in these wants, these limitless wants, at least as perceived, and our needs can never be satisfied in this life because, again, as St. Augustine reminds us, "Our hearts are restless until they rest in you."[47]

Our hearts.

Our hearts.

Ultimately, it is our hearts—our souls—that are restless, not our bodies. Ultimately, it is our hearts—our souls—that are restless, and so resolving this unrest is impossible through the body, through the material means of this life, through consumption of this abundance that appeals but will never completely satisfy.

Satisfy.

This abundance that can never completely satisfy, and which, which, can even inspire hunger, ever greater hunger. Hunger, ever greater hunger and as Jesus reminds us, "Life is more than food, and the body more than clothing."[48] And so we

---

47 St. Augustine, *Confessions.*
48 MT 6:25

have been instructed: "Do not love the world or the things of the world. If anyone loves the world, love for the Father is not in Him. For everything in the world—the lust of the flesh, the lust of the eyes, and the pride of life—comes not from the Father but from the world. The world and its desires pass away, but whoever does the will of God lives forever."[49]

Forever.

Whoever does the will of God lives forever.

Forever.

Forever.

Whoever does the will of God lives forever.

Forever.

Forever.

Forever, this greatest opportunity. Forever, this loftiest prospect. Forever, this most fearsome reality. Forever, this most meaningful, yet perilous challenge, given our treating ourselves, as we do, as mini-deities, as gods of our own, as gods of

49 1 JN 2:15-17

ourselves, as gods of this world, this
ephemeral world, this life, this ephemeral
life, this life in this world that falls so short
of forever, this life in this world in which, as
stated in that great psalm,

> "Seventy is the sum of our years,
> or eighty, if we are strong;
> Most of them are toil and sorrow;
> they pass quickly, and we are

gone."[50]

> Gone.

> Gone.

> They pass quickly, and we are gone.

> Gone.

> Gone.

> Forever.

> Gone, gone from here, and into

forever, itself, the forever-after, forever-after.

> Us, we.

> We, us.

> Gone, into the forever-after.

> Gone, gone from here, into the

forever-after.

> Gone.

---

50 PS 90:10

Gone.

Gone from here.

Gone.

V.

And so it is that the self can snare.
The self can snare through its own actions,
given its weakness and the allure of the
world's abundance. The self can snare,
indeed; and the self can become, itself,
ensnared.

Ensnared.

The self can snare, indeed, and the
self can become, itself, ensnared, by the
world—and by others.

Others.

The self can snare, itself, through its
own actions, given its weakness, and by the
temptation of the world's abundance, and
by, and through, our relations with others.

Others.

Others, because the self is not just

the self in isolation. The self is the self, too, in the great and beautiful complexity that is the self among other selves. The self is itself relative to other selves, to others, because the self is not just the self in isolation, the self is the self among others, because flesh lives among flesh.

It is as He made us.

Flesh lives among flesh, it is as He made us, and so it is good, and though the spirit may be willing the flesh is weak. The flesh—this flesh—is subject to its needs, its own crying needs, its musts, its own crying musts, at least as perceived by the self.

The self.

But the self is not just the self in isolation, because the self lives in the world, and so the self is, necessarily, itself, among, others.

Others.

There are others among ourselves, and in this, in these relations, in the complex dynamism of the resulting relations and structures there is the great potential for love, for love, for love, but also ensnarement.

Ensnarement.

We are, ourselves, truly, when we are among others, living in, society.

Society.

Society.

Society, because we are social, necessarily. Society, because we are social, it is as He made us. Society, because when in this world, it is through our social constructs that we live, daily. It is through our social constructs that we live, daily, and it is through our social constructs, so often imperfect, that we can become ensnared.

Ensnared.

Ensnared.

It is through our social constructs, so often imperfect, that we live, and live, more often than not, imperfectly.

Imperfectly.

It is through our social constructs, so often imperfect, that we live, and live, more often than not, imperfectly, and in this imperfection, in this imperfection where the self, prone to imperfection, lives deeply, profoundly, among the imperfections of these many other selves, in an imperfect society, there is the great potential for the spiraling, warping perversion of Truth that is relativism.

Relativism.

There is the great potential for the spiraling, warping perversion of Truth that is relativism, where right is not necessarily right, and where wrong is not necessarily wrong, where rightness and wrongness is determined by majority, and not necessarily according to His will. This is the imperfection of society's ways.

Society.

This is the imperfection of society's ways.

Society.

And our society, our societies, are not His society.

Our society, our societies, are not His society, just as His ways are not our ways. His ways, are not our ways, and our society is not His society.

But there is just one true society,

His.

There is just one true society, His, and we are to attempt to replicate it with perfection here on earth, because it is written, "thy will be done on earth, as it is in Heaven."

"On earth, as it is in Heaven."

"On earth, as it is in Heaven."

In Heaven's society, there is perfection.

Perfection.

In man's society, there is only the potential for perfection; in reality, in man's society, what we have, so often, is grave imperfection.

Imperfection.

And imperfection encourages imperfection. It is the scourge of relativism, and it is why we are to strive for the opposite, for Truth in perfection, so that perfection among imperfection can temper imperfection, and make what is imperfect perfect.

Perfect.

It is why we are to strive for the

232

opposite, for Truth in perfection, so that perfection among imperfection can temper imperfection, and make what is imperfect perfect.

Perfect.

We are to strive for perfection through holiness, to make what is imperfect perfect, beginning with ourselves, because as Blessed Elizabeth Leseur so wisely noted, "Every soul that uplifts itself uplifts the world."

The world.

The world is, "this age," and we are to protect ourselves from the snares of this age, this age, this sinful age, and St. Paul warns us, "Do not conform yourselves to this age."[51]

This age.

"Do not conform yourselves to this age."

This age.

This age, is the present age. This age, is the present society. This age is this imperfect, imperfect society, in which we

51 ROM 12:2

live, daily. This age, is this imperfect society, where "the god of this age"—the devil, the devil, that most heinous, deviant fiend—"has blinded the minds of the unbelievers, so that they may not see the light of the gospel of the glory of Christ, who is the image of God."[52]

The devil.

The devil.

The devil, the god of this age.

The devil, who ensnares.

The devil, true beast, true ruined, prideful beast.

The devil, true beast, true ruined, prideful beast who seeks the destruction of souls, who uses this age to dupe, who is this age, the god of this age, is in this age, blinding the minds of the unbelievers, warping outlooks, deforming society, because we let him, we let him, by conforming ourselves to this age, and so, as St. Paul wrote, "Do not conform yourselves to this age, but be transformed by the renewal of your mind, that you may discern

---

52 2 COR 4:4

what is the will of God, what is good and pleasing and perfect."[53]

Perfect.

"What is good and pleasing and perfect."

Perfect.

"Do not conform yourselves to this age, [but] discern what is the will of God."

God.

God.

God!

"...discern what is the will of God."

God.

God.

God!

"Do not conform yourselves to this age, [but] discern what is the will of God."

Discern.

Choose.

Choose!

Choose to do His will in this age, this imperfect age, this age, this sinful age, choose to do His will in this age to avoid wickedness and ensnarement.

---

53 ROM 12:2

Ensnarement.

Ensnarement.

Choose to do His will in this age, this age, this muddled age, to avoid the wickedness and ensnarements of this age, this age, this errant, impoverished, and prideful age.

This age, this age—this age that is every age; until He comes.

This age that is every age; until He comes, and so we are to remain steadfast in Him, because "if we persevere, we shall also reign with him. But if we deny him, he will deny us."[54] And so we are not to conform ourselves to this age, this age, this wayward age.

We are, instead, to conform ourselves to His age.

His age.

His timeless age.

We are to conform ourselves, to His age, His age, for life in His society, His timeless, most joyful, most peaceful, most loving society.

---

54 2 TIM 2:12

But how?

How?

How?

How are we to do so?

How are we to conform ourselves, in love, to His age, to His will?

How are we to do His will, "On earth, as it is in Heaven?"

How are we to avoid the snares presented by the body, this most blessed, but corruptible, vessel?

How are we to avoid the snares presented by the mind, this most wondrous, but often prideful, creation?

How are we to not be complicit in the perversion of Truth, the most proud accomplishment of this wicked age?

How are we to avoid the snares of society, and self?

Society, and self.

How are we to avoid the snares of society, and self, and the devil?

Because society, and self, and the devil can snare.

Society, and self, and the devil can

snare.

Snare.

Snare.

Snare.

Society, and self, and the devil can snare.

Snare.

And so how are we to avoid the snares of society, and self and the devil?

How?

How?

How?

How?

VI.

He has given us the means.

He has given us the means, for what good and gracious, and all-powerful father, would not give His children the means to overcome their problems? What good and gracious and all-loving father, would abandon His children to their own fate?

What good and gracious and all-knowing father would not give His children what they need so that they may be united with Him?

Him.

He has given us Himself, and He has given us His word, and He has given us His only Son, and He has given us the wonders and presence of His Holy Spirit, and He has given us our holy mother church, and He has given us the sacraments, and He has given us prayer, and He has given us His holy mother, and the example of the saints, and He has given us the capacity for virtue.

Virtue.

He has given us the capacity for virtue, so that we may access all these good things He has given us, and access them perfectly.

Perfectly.
Perfectly, through our virtue.
Virtue.
Perfectly, through our virtue.
Virtue.

He has given us the capacity for virtue, so that we may access all these good things that will ensure our future with Him.

Him.

Virtue.

Our virtue, we control, through Him.

Through Him, we control, our virtue.

Our virtue, we control, through Him, and thus we control our lives, we control our fate, through our virtue.

Virtue.

We control our fate, through Him, through our virtue.

Our virtue.

Our virtue.

Virtue.

Virtue.

Virtue, the means by which we access all these good things. Virtue, the means by which we avoid ensnarement. Virtue, the means by which we purify ourselves, and appeal for His grace in our lives.

Virtue.

These seven virtues: Faith, Hope, Love; Justice, Prudence, Temperance, Fortitude. That is it.

That is it.

These seven virtues.

That is it.

This is it.

Virtue.

These seven virtues, given to us.

These seven virtues, given to us so that we may access these others great gifts.

These seven virtues, given to us so that through their employment we may appeal for His grace.

His grace.

His grace.

His grace, our salve, the answer to our ache, our ache, our incomparable ache.

Our ache, our ache, our incomparable ache.

He loves us. He who is love. He loves us. He has given us Himself, His son, His Holy Spirit, His church, His sacraments, His holy mother, the saints, prayer, and He has given us the capacity for virtue.

Virtue.

He has given us the capacity for virtue so that we may access these other great gifts, and so that we may appeal for His grace.

His grace.

His grace.

Our salve, His grace.

His grace, His grace, His efficacious grace.

His grace, His grace, the end of all matters.

The end, His grace. The only good end, His grace. Our salve, Him, by His grace, because His grace is Him. Him. His grace is Him.

Him.

His grace is Him, our salve.

We appeal for His grace through our virtue.

Our virtue.

We appeal for the only salve to our ache through our virtue.

Our virtue.

We appeal for the only salve to our
ache through our virtue.

Our virtue.

Through our virtue.

Our virtue.

Our virtue.

Our virtue.

Virtue.

We appeal for the only salve to our
ache through our virtue.

Through our, virtue.

IV.   Virtue

I.

And so *Virtue!*

Virtue!

Virtue, so it is!

So it is, virtue!

Virtue!

Virtue.

Virtue, no stone, no water, no sky,
no sun.

Virtue, no person, no family, no
country, no world.

Virtue.

Virtue.

Virtue, so it is.

So it is, virtue.

Virtue.

Virtue.

Virtue, because as Pope Leo XIII said, "Virtue, and virtue alone, wherever found, will be followed by the rewards of everlasting happiness."[55]

Virtue, and virtue alone!

Virtue, and virtue alone, wherever found, will be followed by the rewards of everlasting happiness.

Virtue, and virtue alone.

Virtue, and virtue alone.

Virtue, and virtue alone, wherever found, will be followed by the rewards of everlasting happiness.

Everlasting happiness.

What else is there, what else could there possibly be, but everlasting happiness?

Everlasting happiness.

What else is there, what else could there possibly be, but everlasting happiness, to be gained by virtue and virtue alone?

Virtue.

Virtue!

Virtue, and virtue alone.

Everlasting happiness—the only

---

55 Pope Leo XIII, *Rerum Novarum.*

good end, the only good outcome—through virtue.

Virtue.

Virtue.

Everlasting happiness through virtue, through virtue, because everlasting happiness is not automatic. Everlasting happiness is not automatic, because virtue is not automatic. Virtue is a choice. A choice. Virtue is a choice, and thus everlasting happiness is a choice. Virtue is a decision, and thus everlasting happiness is a decision. Virtue, is a choice. Virtue, is a decision. And so everlasting happiness is a choice, and everlasting happiness is a decision. Resulting from our virtue.

Virtue.

Virtue, according to Pope Leo, is "the common inheritance of men."[56]

Virtue, according to the catechism, is our opportunity "to become like God."[57]

Virtue, according to St. Augustine, is "the good exercise of free-will."[58]

---

56 Pope Leo XIII, *Rerum Novarum*.

57 *Catechism of the Catholic Church*, 1803.

58 St. Augustine, *On Free Will*, 2.19.

247

Free-will.

Free-will.

Virtue, the good exercise of free-will. Free-will; because our will is free. Our will is free to do as it pleases, in this ultimate act of love, God's love. Freedom. This ultimate act of love, God's love. Freedom. Because love, true love, is a decision, a choice. Love, true love, is a decision, a choice, and we can choose to love truly, and we can choose to not. True love, is a choice. And love, is a virtue.

Virtue.

Love, is a virtue, "the greatest of these."[59]

Love.

Virtue. Love. Love is a virtue. "The greatest of these." Love. The virtue of love. We do not, as humans, simply love; we draw from that wellspring of love within us and employ the virtue of love. It is easy, or it is hard. We are successful, or we fail, depending on the depth of love within us.

Love.

---

59 1 COR 13:13

Love is a virtue, "the greatest of these." Love, true love, is a choice, based in our free-will, because our will is free. Our will is free to do as it pleases, in the ultimate act of love, God's love.

Freedom.

The ultimate act of love, God's love.

Freedom.

Because love, true love, is a decision, a choice. But in this liberty, in this freedom, in this power, in this choice we can become lost, or disillusioned, or confused, or prideful. We can become ensnared.

Ensnared.

In this liberty, in this freedom, in this power, in this choice, we can lose our way, and become, ensnared.

Ensnared.

Ensnared, but then there is virtue.

Virtue.

Ensnared, but then there is virtue, virtue, to guide us in our acting freely, to direct us in our choices, to make us firm, to make us resolute, to make us stable, to

make us good, to order our passions, to
master our selves, to perfect our nature, to
infuse us with joy, to overcome evil, to love
what is right, to despise what is wrong, to
root us in goodness, to make us noble, to
make us worthy.

Worthy.

To make us worthy.

Worthy.

To make us worthy of the promises
of Christ.

What else could there possibly be?

What else could there possibly be
but to be worthy of the promises of Christ?

The promises of Christ is life
everlasting. What else could there possibly
be?

No stone, no water, no sky, no sun.

What else could there possibly be?

No person, no family, no country,
no world.

What else could there possibly be?

What else could there possibly be
but to be worthy of the promises of Christ,
because the promises of Christ is life itself,

life, true life, life everlasting, and it goes no
further, and it gets no better, and nothing
exceeds it, life, true life, and we get there,
through virtue.

Virtue.

We get there, through virtue.

Virtue.

We get there, through virtue, and so
it is, virtue.

Virtue, so it is.

Virtue.

Virtue, and virtue alone.

Virtue.

Virtue.

Virtue, and virtue alone, to receive
the promises of Christ, life.

Virtue.

We get there through virtue.

Virtue.

We get there

through virtue.

II.

And so it is, virtue; but virtue, what
is it?

It.

What is it?

It.

It.

It is Faith.

It is Hope.

It is Love.

Virtue.

It is Temperance.

It is Prudence.

It is Justice.

It is Fortitude.

Virtue.

That is it. These seven virtues.
One informing the others, the others
informing all. Virtue.

Virtue.

That is it. These seven virtues.

These seven virtues.

But how do we get there? How do we know it? How do we live it?

We get there, through virtue itself. We know it, through virtue itself. We live it, through virtue itself. And only through Him.

Virtue.

Virtue rooted in God, the Father. Virtue rooted in Jesus Christ, the Son. Virtue rooted in the most Holy Spirit.

Virtue.

Virtue, this way, is the way, is the only way, because rooted in Him, He who is, He who is the beginning, He who is the ending, is the way, the only way, the only possible way, this way.

Virtue.

This way, virtue. This way, is practical. Virtue, is practical. Virtue, is practical, because virtue is *the* way, the only way. And so virtue is the only form of practicality, if practicality is a means to an end, the end, the ultimate end, the only end that matters.

Virtue.

Virtue.

Because virtue is, just as He is.

But are we just, virtuous? No, we are not just, virtuous. We are not just, virtuous, though virtue, is our nature. Virtue, is our nature, because virtue is good and we were created good, because we were created in His image, and He is good, the ultimate good, and so we were not created bad, but good, and so virtue, is our nature.

Our nature.

Virtue is, our nature, and we are created good. We are created good and we are pre-disposed to virtue because virtue is the essence of a life. We cannot live a life, a human life, without indulging, or neglecting, virtue.

Virtue.

Virtue is, just as He is. And so we are virtue, we *are* our virtue.

We *are* our virtue.

We *are* our virtue, and by our virtue will we be judged. By our virtue will we be judged because "virtue, and virtue alone will be followed by the rewards of everlasting happiness."[60]

Virtue, and virtue alone.

Everlasting happiness.

Everlasting happiness, resulting from our virtue.

Our virtue.

Our virtue.

And though we are predisposed to virtue, we are not just virtuous. Virtue is a choice. Virtue is a goal. Virtue is an effort. Virtue is real. Virtue is an act. Virtue is a state of being. Virtue is doing. Virtue is living. Virtue is us, we *are* our virtue. We *are* our virtue, but how do we become virtuous?

How do we?

How do we?

How do we become virtuous?

The answer is: through Him.

Through Him, God the Father, because from Him all good things come.

Through Him, Jesus Christ, because no one goes to the Father except through

---

60 Pope Leo XIII, *Rerum Novarum.*

Him.

Through Him, the Holy Spirit, because the seven gifts of the Holy Spirit "complete and perfect the virtues of those who receive them."[61]

Through Him, with Him, and in Him, because the goal of life, a practical life, the only life to be aspired, the only life to live, is the virtuous life. The virtuous life, through Him.

The virtuous life, through Him.

The virtuous life through Him, with Him, and in Him.

The virtuous life.

The virtuous life.

Virtue.

Virtue.

The only life to be aspired.

The virtuous life.

61 *Catechism of the Catholic Church*, 1831.

Virtue, but practicality is a process,
because one is not just practical, just as one
is not just virtuous. One is not just
practical, without first understanding what
practical is. One is not just practical,
particularly when self and society and the
devil can snare. One is not just practical,
because practicality is a process, a
distillation, a simplification, a purification, a
devotion and then, ultimately, a gush.

A gush!

A gush of humility, a gush of
awareness of Him, a gush of self-awareness,
awareness of our poverty, a gush of
reverence, a gush of understanding, a gush
of joy, a gush of love.

Love!

Practicality leads to love's gush,
love's most unfathomable gush, because
practicality, when taken to its logical end,

leads only to God, who is the only end, and "God is love."[62]

Love.

"God is love," that most perfect love. "God is love," and practicality is a process. Practicality is prudence. Prudence.

Prudence.

Practicality is prudence. Practicality is prudence and prudence is a virtue. Practicality is prudence, and prudence is "the mother of all virtues." Practicality is prudence, and prudence leads us, practically, to Him.

Him.

To Him.

Prudence.

Prudence leads us, to Him, because prudence enables us to know what to desire, and to know what to avoid. And that is life, the first step toward life. And that is life, the first step of many toward life, true life. Desire the good, avoid the bad. It is innate, but it must be rooted, it must be nurtured, it must be developed—but first it must be

---

62 1 JN 4:8

known!

Known.

It must be known.

Known.

First it must be known, because
what is the good, if we have never been
told? And what is the bad, if we have never
been told? And what is the Truth, if we
have never been told? And how will we live
properly, if we have never been told? And
how will we make that final step into life,
true life, if we have never been told in
which direction true life lies? How? How?
How?

And so exposure to the Truth is the
beginning of prudence.

Prudence.

Exposure to the Truth is the
beginning of prudence.

Prudence.

And so exposure to the Truth is
true life's rich soil, without which true life
cannot take root, because as Jesus said,
"Some [seed] fell on rocky ground, where it
had little soil. It sprang up at once because

the soil was not deep, and when the sun rose it was scorched, and it withered for lack of roots...But some seed fell on rich soil, and produced fruit, a hundred or sixty or thirtyfold."[63]

That rich soil is our exposure to the Truth, and exposure to the Truth is the beginning of prudence.

Prudence.

Exposure to the Truth is the beginning of prudence, the beginning of knowledge, the beginning of wisdom, the beginning of discernment—the beginning of knowing what to desire and what to avoid.

The beginning.

Exposure to the Truth is the beginning of prudence, but what of prudence's middle, and what of prudence's end? A seed in rich soil will grow and produce fruit, but we are not seeds, because seeds do not have free-will.

Free-will.

Seeds do not have free-will, but

---

63 MT 13:3-9

humans do, and humans can accept or reject that rich soil. Prudence's beginning is exposure to the Truth, and so the beginning of prudence is our Baptism, our first exposure—and our continued exposure—to the faith. This is life's rich soil. This exposure is life's rich soil, but we can reject Truth's nutrients, or we can ingest them. We can reject Truth's nutrients or we can ingest them; ingesting Truth's nutrients brings us to prudence's middle, our accepting the Truth. Prudence's middle is our accepting the Truth, and growing in that rich soil.

Soil.

Prudence's middle is our accepting the Truth, and growing in that rich soil.

Soil.

Prudence's ending is our living the Truth, as we burst into the light of life. Prudence's ending is our living the Truth, as we burst into the light of life. Prudence's ending is our true beginning.

Our true beginning.

Prudence's ending is our true

beginning, but a true beginning is far from ensured.

Ensured.

Because we can become ensnared.

Ensnared.

A true beginning is far from ensured because prudence is a virtue, and virtue is a choice of free-will. Prudence is a virtue, a choice of free-will and our prudence is shallow or deep.

Our prudence is shallow or deep.

Shallow prudence is imprudence. Shallow prudence is making decisions from a rootless base. Shallow prudence is losing sight of eternal life, is losing sight of needing to make every decision in light of it. Prudence informs the rest of our virtue. It is our base. It is our base.

Prudence is our base, and so it is, *prudence!*

Prudence, so it is.

Prudence, knowledge rooted.

Prudence, wisdom lived.

Prudence, enabling us to see and hear and think.

Prudence, enabling us to make right
choices.

Prudence, our base.

Prudence, our good roots in rich
soil, without which we scorch and whither.

Prudence.

Prudence, our good roots in rich
soil.

Prudence.

Prudence, so it is.

So it is, prudence.

Prudence.

Prudence.

Prudence, so it is.

So it is, prudence.

IV.

Prudence.

Prudence.

But what is prudence, without faith?

There can be no prudence, without
faith.

There can be no prudence, without faith because prudence, true prudence, is making life's decisions in light of the Truth.

But the Truth is seen, and the Truth is unseen.

The Truth is seen, and the Truth is unseen.

Prudence merely knows, and then acts. Prudence, rooted in knowledge, can only truly know that which can be seen. And so prudence cannot truly know that which cannot be seen. And so prudence relies on faith, and "faith is the substance of things hoped for; the evidence of things not seen."[64]

And so faith is evidence; spiritual evidence necessary for the virtue of prudence.

Prudence.

And so prudence, true prudence, is only prudence in faith.

Faith.

Prudence, true prudence, is only prudence in faith.

---

64 HEB 11:1

Faith.

Faith, "the fundamental act of our Christian existence."[65]

Faith, God's living breath within us.

Faith, "so that whoever believes in Him shall have eternal life."[66]

Faith, belief.

Faith, so that man may hope, because "what a man seeth, what doth he hope for?"[67]

Faith. "For by grace you are saved through faith—and this is not from yourselves, for it is the gift of God."[68]

Faith, "the gift of God."

Faith, "the gift of God," granted to those who believe.

Faith, the realization of belief.

Faith, knowledge—concrete knowledge—of the Truth, even the Truth that cannot be seen, because faith is "the gift of God," and God's gifts are real, not unreal, and so faith is real knowledge of the

65 Pope Benedict XVI, *Christianity and the Crisis of Cultures.*

66 JN 3:16

67 ROM 8:24

68 EPH 2:8

Truth that cannot be seen.

Faith.

And so faith is real, the concrete and real knowledge of that which cannot be seen.

Faith.

Faith is real, because the Truth is real, and because the Truth cannot be unreal.

Faith is real, because the Truth is real, and because the Truth cannot be unreal.

Faith is real, and it makes men like God, and its absence reduces men to less than beasts, because again, as it is written, "Now ask the beasts to teach you, and the birds of the air to tell you; or the reptiles on earth to instruct you, and the fish of the sea to inform you. Which of all these does not know that the hand of God has done this? In his hand is the soul of every living thing, and the life breath of all mankind."[69]

Yes, but still, "This generation is an evil generation; it seeks a sign, but no sign

69 JOB 12:7-10

will be given it, except the sign of Jonah."[70]
And the sign of Jonah was real! Nineveh
was saved! The sign of Jonah was real!
Nineveh was saved! And so in his mercy
and love, a sign has been given, even to
those of little faith.

>Faith.
>
>Faith is real.
>
>Faith, so it is.
>
>And so faith it is.
>
>Faith.
>
>Faith.
>
>Faith is real.
>
>And so it is.
>
>And so faith it is.
>
>Faith.
>
>Faith.
>
>And from faith springs hope.
>
>Hope!

There can be no hope—true hope,
hope in the Truth—without faith—true
faith, faith in the Truth; and in turn, faith
in the truth brings hope.

>*Hope!*

70 LK 11:29-30

Faith in the Truth brings hope, because in faith there is an objective, in faith there is a reward, in faith there is belief in the only outcome that matters, our eternal outcome, and in faith, and with faith, and through faith, a living faith, that eternal outcome—unmitigated, unsurpassed peace and joy and love—will be achieved.

Unmitigated, unsurpassed peace and joy and love!

What else is there? What else could there possibly be? What else could we aspire to? What else is as good? What else is as fulfilling?

What else?

What else?

What else?

Mitigated peace?

Partial joy?

Occasional love?

In other words, the modest offerings of this present world?

No. There is only the excellence of faith's reward to be aspired to, and so in faith we have hope, and "we are saved by hope. But hope that is seen is not hope. For what a man seeth, what doth he hope for? But if we hope for that which we do not see, we wait for it with patience."[71]

Patience.

Hope.

Hope enables patience, just as faith enables hope. Hope enables patience just as faith enables hope. We have hope because we have faith, true faith, and in faith there is reward. In faith there is reward, and it can be no other way. It can be no other way because faith without reward would be foolish. If there was no reward, no objective, no good outcome, what good would faith be?

Be.

Be.

If there was no reward, no objective, no good outcome, what good would faith be? But in faith, true faith, there is reward, and because there is reward—the ultimate reward, the only reward that matters—we have hope.

---

71 ROM 8:24-5

Hope.

We have hope because we have faith, true faith, and in faith there is reward, not just in the future, but now.

Now.

Now.

Hope.

Hope is now.

Hope is faith's present reward.

Hope.

Now.

Hope is now.

Hope is faith's present reward, because hope is not passive, hope is active, in the present, in the now, and it is just as Pope Benedict XVI said: "The one who has hope lives differently."[72]

Differently.

"The one who has hope lives differently," and in living differently, hope is active. Hope is not passive, but active, because in faith we know that "we are saved by hope."

Hope.

72 Pope Benedict XVI, *Spe Salvi*.

Hope.

We are saved by hope.

Hope.

Hope.

Hope, and "the one who has hope lives differently."

Differently.

Hope, and "the one who has hope lives differently."

Differently.

And isn't that our calling, to live differently? Isn't that as we have been instructed, to live differently? We are to live differently. We are to live differently, because "narrow is the path and the few that find it."[73] We are to live differently, so that we may find it. We are to live differently, because "many are called but few are chosen."[74] We are to live differently, so that we may be chosen. We are to live differently, because "the harvest is plentiful, but the laborers are few."[75] We are to live differently, so that we may be

---

73 MT 7:14

74 MT 22:14

75 MT 9:37

271

among the few.

The few.

The few among Him; *and oh, to be among those few!*

The few. To be among those few!

The few among Him, to be among those few.

This is our hope.

Hope.

This is our hope.

Hope.

This is our hope, to be among those few.

To be among those few.

Those few.

To be among those few, this is our hope.

Hope.

Our hope, our hope, Jesus Christ, our hope.

Hope.

Our hope, our hope, Jesus Christ, our hope.

Hope.

Jesus Christ, the object of our hope.

Hope.

Hope.

Hope, in Jesus Christ, savior.

Savior. Savior of all nations. Our savior.

Savior. Jesus Christ. Our savior. Saving. Us. We, us. Saved. We are saved. "We are saved by hope." We are saved by hope, and we are saved by Jesus Christ, and so Jesus Christ is hope.

Hope.

Jesus Christ is hope.

Hope.

Jesus Christ is hope.

Hope.

Jesus Christ is hope, and if we have hope, true hope, we have Jesus Christ.

Jesus Christ.

If we have hope, true hope, we have Jesus Christ.

Jesus Christ.

If we have hope, true hope, we have Jesus Christ.

Jesus Christ.

Jesus the Christ.

Hope.

Jesus Christ.

Hope.

What else could there possibly be to have but Jesus Christ?

What else?

What else could there possibly be to have?

What else could there possibly be?

What else?

What else could there possibly be to have?

What else?

What else, and so hope saves!

Hope.

Hope saves!

Hope.

Hope saves, because in living with hope, "Everyone who has this hope, based on him, makes himself pure, as he is pure."[76]

Pure.

Purity.

Perfection. Purity, true purity, is perfection.

---

76 1 JN 3:3

Perfection.

Purity.

Pure.

It is what He wants, it is what He expects.

We make ourselves pure through our hope.

We make ourselves pure through our hope, and because of our hope; because of our hope, we seek to make ourselves pure, to be like Him, to be appealing to Him, to appeal to Him, so that we may be with Him.

Because of our hope.

Because of our hope—true hope, hope in the Truth—and through our virtue.

Virtue.

We appeal to Him, because of our hope, through our virtue.

Virtue.

We appeal to Him, through our virtue.

Virtue.

Virtue, through the active virtue in our lives.

Virtue.

We appeal to Him through the active virtue in our lives, in our seeking Him, in our supplication, in our urging Him down to us, in our seeking to ascend to Him, through our Faith and Hope, and by our Love, which powers all.

All.

All.

By our love, which powers all.

All.

All.

We appeal to Him through the purification of our earthly selves, through the active virtues in our earthly lives, through the active virtues that purify us, that make us pure, that make us perfect, perfect, perfect, and we do it through our Prudence, and through our Temperance, and through our Justice, and through our Fortitude, rooted in Faith, and inspired by Hope, and by our Love, which powers all, which powers all. And by our Love, which powers all.

All.

All.

By our love, which powers all.

All.

All.

All.

...but wait!

Wait!

Wait.

Love awaits, love's discussion
awaits.

Awaits.

Awaits.

Love's discussion awaits, this love
that powers all.

All.

This love, the beginning, the
ending, this love that powers all.

All.

And so hope saves, and inspires us
to purify our earthly selves, because
"everyone who has this hope, based on him,
makes himself pure, as he is pure."[77]

And we purify ourselves by
obtaining His grace, which we appeal for
through prayer and through the sacraments
and through the virtues, the virtues of faith,

---

77 1 JN 3:3

hope and love, of fortitude, justice,
temperance and prudence. And prudence
brought us here.

Prudence.

Prudence brought us here, to this
beginning, because prudence's ending is our
true beginning, our true beginning.
Prudence's ending is our true beginning,
our true beginning, but what is prudence
without faith?

Faith.

What is prudence without faith?

Faith.

What is prudence without faith,
"the substance of things hoped for; the
evidence of things not seen."[78]

Faith.

And from faith springs hope, and
hope saves, because "everyone who has this
hope, based on him, makes himself pure, as
he is pure."[79]

And we make ourselves pure
through virtue.

Virtue.

We make ourselves pure through
virtue.

---

78 HEB 11:1
79 1 JN 3:3

Virtue.

And so prudence brought us here, to this new beginning, prudence enabled by faith, from which hope springs forth, and which leads to love, true love, the only true love, love based in Truth, love based in Him, love based in Truth.

Truth.

Truth.

And so prudence brought us here, where we are now, here, here, prudence brought us here, prudence, the mother of all virtues, of the cardinal virtues, the mother of fortitude, of temperance and justice.

Fortitude, temperance, and justice.

Fortitude, temperance, and justice.

Fortitude, temperance, and justice.

V.

A lion, a wheel, a scale.

Fortitude, temperance, and justice.

A lion, a wheel, a scale.

So real, so real.

A lion, a wheel, a scale.

Look, and see, and touch.
Look, and see, and touch.
So real, so real.
So real, because it needs to be.
Because how will you do it here?
How will you do it under this sky?
How will you do it with feet held
down to this earth?

How will you do it in the midst of
all this, of all these bodies hiding souls,
mixing and repelling, one way and the next?

How will you do it here?

How will you do it here, soul
inhabiting this body?

How will you do it here, soul
inhabiting this need, this crying need?

This need, this crying need. This
need, this need crying out for this sky,
crying out for this earth; this need crying
out for this sky that never ends; this need
crying out for this earth that never fulfills.

How will you do it here, in practice?

How will you do it here, with
breath?

How will you do it here?

Here.

How will you do it here, where life's gravity pins.

How will you do it here, where there is no escape to someplace else.

Here, where there is no escape to someplace else.

Else.

Someplace else.

Else.

Here where there is no escape to someplace else because there is no other place, but here.

Here.

There is no other place, here.

Here.

There is only here.

And so how will you do it here?

How will you do it here, under this sky, and with feet held down to this earth?

How?

How?

Through virtue.

Virtue.

Through fortitude, strength.

Through temperance, control.

Through justice, care.

Fortitude, temperance, justice.

Fortitude, temperance, justice.

Under the guidance of prudence,
the mother of all virtues; prudence enabled
by faith; faith inspiring hope; and love, love;
love, true love, love, true love, which powers
all.

Fortitude.

Temperance.

Justice.

Fortitude.

Temperance.

Justice.

VI.

And so fortitude.

Fortitude.

Fortitude, the lion, because what
can we do without strength?

Fortitude, the lion, because

prudence can falter without resolve, and temperance is unattainable without firmness, and justice becomes secondary without courage.

Fortitude.

Fortitude.

Fortitude, because we are to "consider it all joy when [we] encounter various trials."[80]

Fortitude, because "the testing of [our] faith produces perseverance."[81]

Fortitude, because we are to "let perseverance be perfect, so that [we] may be perfect and complete."[82]

Perfect.

"Let perseverance be perfect."

Perfect.

"Let perseverance be perfect," and perseverance is fortitude, and so let fortitude be perfect.

Perfect.

Let fortitude be perfect so that we may be perfect, because perfection of

---

80 JAMES 1:2-4

81 JAMES 1:2-4

82 JAMES 1:2-4

fortitude—true fortitude, fortitude in the
Truth—will ensure that any challenge to
our eternity with Him can be overcome.

Fortitude.

Let fortitude be perfect.

Perfect.

Let fortitude be perfect.

Perfect.

Let fortitude be perfect because as
St. Francis de Sales said, fortitude "is the
most desirable virtue in the spiritual life.
We are forever changing...My God, what a
shame that we are so inconstant! Surely,
there is no stability in us, and yet this is the
most essential quality in the spiritual life."[83]

Fortitude.

Fortitude, the most essential quality
in the spiritual life, because without it we
are just reeds bending in the wind. Without
fortitude there can be no true spiritual life,
because a spiritual life is a sacrificing life,
and there can be no sacrificing without
fortitude.

Fortitude.

---

83 *Magnificat*, "Meditation of the Day," 12/11/10.

There can be no true spiritual life, a life of sacrifice, without fortitude. And with no true spiritual life there can be no eternal life.

Eternal life.

There can be no eternal life without fortitude in this life, because this earthly life is arduous and difficult and filled with temptation, and how easy it is to acquiesce! How easy it is to acquiesce—*to be among the many!* How hard it is to be constant, and righteous—*to be among the few!*

The few.

The few.

How hard it is to be among the few, but we "can do all this in Him who gives [us] strength."[84]

Strength.

We can do all this in Him, who gives us strength.

Strength.

Strength, because "Whatever we do, the world will wage war on us."[85]

Strength, because "Whatever we do,

---

84 PHIL 4:13

85 St. Francis de Sales, *Introduction to the Devout Life*, Section 4.1.

the world will wage war on us, and so let us be firm in our purpose and unwavering in our resolutions."[86]

Strength.

Strength.

Strength to be firm in our purpose, unwavering in our resolutions, and as Jesus said, "If the world hates you, realize that it hated me first.[87]"

Strength.

Strength.

Strength revealed through fortitude.

Fortitude, and once we learn it, we can withstand any trial, because as Jesus said, "My yoke is easy, my burden light."[88]

Light.

Light.

"My yoke is easy, my burden light," with fortitude.

Fortitude.

Fortitude, because strength overcomes suffering. In this world, in this fallen world, there is suffering. Strength

---

86 St. Francis de Sales, *Introduction to the Devout Life*, Section 4.1.
87 JN 15:18
88 MT 11:30

overcomes suffering, and is made possible through hope.

Hope.

Strength—true strength, strength in the Truth—is only possible through hope.

Hope.

Strength is only possible through hope, because why else would we suffer? Why else would we suffer unless we have Him?

Him.

Him.

Why else would we suffer unless we have Him, He who shows us that the suffering body is meaningless?

Him.

He who said, "I tell you, my friends, do not be afraid of those who kill the body but after that can do no more. I shall show you whom to fear. Be afraid of the one who after killing has the power to cast into Gehenna."[89]

Gehenna!

Hell!

---

89 LK 12:4-5

Hell!

Gehenna!

That there is a hell, that there is such a place, that it is real, that such a place awaits us if we live this life in weakness.

Weakness.

That such a place awaits us if we live this life in weakness and inconstancy, in weakness and without resolve, in weakness and without fidelity. In weakness.

Weakness.

In spiritual weakness.

That such a place awaits us if we live this life in weakness; but we can avoid this place, can avoid the devil's temptations through strength, through fortitude.

Through fortitude.

Fortitude.

We avoid the devil's temptations and receive the grace of the Father through fortitude.

Fortitude.

We avoid the devil's temptations and receive the grace of the Father through fortitude.

Fortitude.

Fortitude.

Through fortitude, because "they that hope in the Lord shall renew their strength, they shall take wings as eagles, they shall run and not be weary, they shall walk and not faint."[90]

And what else is there, what else might there be?

What else?

What else is there, what else might there be?

What might there be?

Be?

Be?

"I love you, Lord, my strength!"[91]

VII.

My strength.

My strength.

"I love you, Lord, my strength."

---

90 IS 40:31
91 PS 18:2

Strength not in might, but in what might be.

Strength not in might, but in what should be...and in what should not be.

Should not be.

Should not be.

Strength, that essence of Christian strength, that essence that is not glowering, glaring dominance, but humility and meekness and restraint and modesty and control.

Control.

Control, because look at all there is.

Control, because look at all there is.

All this.

All this!

Look at all there is.

All this.

All this!

All this, this fertile world. All this, this immeasurable depth. All this, love's downfall or love's opportunity.

All this.

All this.

And how do we know all this? We

know all this because it is before us. We
know all this because it is as He made us.
We are aware of all this through our mind
and through our senses. We experience all
this through our thinking and through our
acting. But we are to be careful, because
our knowledge, and our awareness, and our
thinking, and our acting has implications
for our spirit.

Our spirit.

These things we encounter and
experience through the body effect our
spirit.

Our spirit.

We are able to experience all this
through our feeling body, through the
immediacy of our feeling body, and our
actions affect our sentient spirit.

Our spirit.

Our sentient spirit.

Our body.

The actions of our body, the
reactions of our body to all this effects our
spirit, our sentient spirit.

Our sentient spirit miraculously

291

entwined with our body.

Our body.

Our sentient spirit miraculously
entwined with our body, but we are to be
aware, because the body is easily corrupted,
corrupting the spirit. The body is easily
corrupted, corrupting the spirit. The body
is easily corrupted and we are to be careful
and aware because as we have been told: "if
you live according to the flesh, you will die,
but if by the spirit you put to death the
deeds of the body, you will live."[92]

You will live.

If by the spirit you put to death the
deeds of the body, you will live. Live. And
to live we must die to ourselves, because as
Paul said, "I live, no longer I, but Christ
lives in me; insofar as I now live in the
flesh, I live by faith in the Son of God who
has loved me and given himself up for
me."[93]

But the body is powerful, and it is
first to experience all this.

All this.

---

92 ROM 8:13
93 GAL 2:20

The body is powerful and it is the first to experience all this, but the body must be controlled. The body must be controlled by the body first, but then by the spirit.

By the spirit.

The body must be controlled by the body first, but then by the spirit because "the one who sows for his flesh will reap corruption from the flesh, but the one who sows for the spirit will reap eternal life from the spirit."[94]

Eternal life.

From the spirit.

For the spirit.

For the future.

But for the now, there is all this.

All this.

All this, available to the body, but impacting the soul.

All this, given by God.

All this, given by God—but to be used according to His will.

His will.

94 GAL 6:8

His will, because there are no bad things but only bad uses of good things. There are no bad things, but only bad uses of good things; bad thoughts, and bad intentions, and bad actions corrupt good things. We are good things; and thus we are able to become corrupted. Good things corrupted is the work of the world, and the work of the devil.[95] Giving in to this corruption is the work of ourselves.

Ourselves.

Giving in to this corruption is the work of ourselves.

Ourselves.

We give in to this corruption through our own will, or through our lack of it.

And it is easy. It is easy, because there is all this.

All this.

It is easy, because there is all this.

All this.

And there are all these occasions, to abuse all this.

95 G.K. Chesterton, *St. Thomas Aquinas*.

All this.

All there are all these occasions, to
abuse all this.

All this.

All these.

All this; **all this!**

And all these.

These occasions.

These occasions.

These occasions to give in to
corruption, to become corrupt, to become
corrupted.

To sin.

These occasions.

To sin.

For sin, to sin.

Sin.

Sin.

Sin.

These occasions for sin, to sin, with
our body, with our mind.

Sin.

This occasion to sin, our body.

This occasion to sin, our mind.

These occasions.

These occasions.

These occasions, us, we.

We, us.

Us, we, these occasions.

To touch.

And taste.

And think.

And feel.

These occasions, us.

Us, these occasions. We are these occasions.

We, this conglomeration of parts.

Parts.

Parts of wonder.

Parts of majesty.

Parts in His image.

But parts that can be corrupted.

Parts that can be corrupted, that can be used as "weapons for wickedness;"[96] because this is how we first live, through our bodies, through our selves, and our bodies have the potential for wickedness.

Wickedness.

Wickedness through our parts; our

---

96 ROM 6:13

parts that are to be used, instead, as "weapons for righteousness,"[97] weapons for righteousness so that we may be raised from the dead to life.

To life.

So that we may be raised from the dead to life, remembering that "Sin must not reign over your mortal bodies so that you obey their desires.[98]"

Desires.

Sin.

Our body is desires.

Desires.

Our body is desires and thus subject to sin.

Our body is desires and thus subject to sin, and so we are to control our body, and control our desires, because to not do this in accordance with His will is to sin, and "the wages of sin is death."[99]

Death.

Death from our desires.

The wages of sin is death, and we

97 ROM 6:13

98 ROM 6:12

99 ROM 6:23

can die from recklessly indulging our desires, but we are to remember "to reject godless ways and worldly desires and to live temperately, justly, and devoutly in this age, as we await the blessed hope, the appearance of the glory of the great God and of our savior Jesus Christ."[100]

Temperately, justly and devoutly.

Temperately.

Temperately, controlling our desires.

We are to live temperately.

We are to live temperately.

We are to have temperance.

Temperance.

We are to have temperance.

Temperance.

We are to live temperately.

Temperately.

We are to have temperance.

Temperance.

We are to have temperance.

And temperance is a virtue.

Temperance is a virtue.

100 TITUS 2:11-13

Temperance is a virtue, a cardinal virtue.

Temperance is a virtue and shares good roots with all other virtues.

Fortitude: temperance is its own form of fortitude—it is strength in controlling our desires.

Prudence: temperance is its own form of prudence—it is wisdom in knowing how much is enough.

Justice: temperance is its own form of justice—it is not taking for ourselves what belongs to others.

Temperance.

Temperance.

We are "to live temperately, justly and devoutly."[101]

In this age.

In this age.

In this "wicked and adulterous age."[102]

In this wicked and adulterous age, where a most prolific offense to our salvation might be the one we are most

---

101 TITUS 2:12
102 MT 12:39

encouraged to indulge without regard: carnality.

Carnality.

Carnality.

Carnality, but we are to live temperately, chastely.

Chastely.

We are to live chastely, because "this most unpopular of Christian virtues"[103] is also "the lily of the virtues, making men nearly the equal of the angels."[104]

Of the angels!

Chastity is of the angels.

Of the angels.

Chastity is of the angels.

Chastity, temperance.

Chastity, temperance, because "this is the will of God, your sanctification; that you should abstain from fornication."[105]

Chastity, temperance, because "fornication, and all uncleanness or covetousness, let it not so much as be

---

103 C.S. Lewis, *Mere Christianity*.

104 St. Francis de Sales, *Introduction to the Devout Life*, 3.12.

105 1 TH 4:3

named among you, as becometh saints."[106]

As becometh saints!

Saints.

As becometh saints.

As becometh saints is perfection.

Perfection.

As becometh saints with regard to chastity is perfection, and we are to remember that "no fornicator, or unclean, or covetous person hath inheritance in the kingdom of Christ and of God."[107]

And so we are to live temperately, and chastely.

And we are to control our desires, with regard to the flesh, to the desire for the flesh of others. We are to live temperately, and chastely.

We are to live chastely, and temperately.

We are to live with control, over our appetites, carnal and other. And other.

Other.

Other.

Other, because we are these needs,

---

106 EPH 5:3

107 Eph 5:3,5

301

these crying needs, and we are to control
our needs so that our needs do not control
us.

Control.

Temperance.

Control.

Temperance.

We are to control ourselves, our
desires, our appetites. We are to put on our
new selves. We are to reject godless ways
and worldly desires. We are to control our
impulses, because "He who keeps the law
controls his impulses."[108]

And we are to keep the law, because
we will live by the law or we will die by the
law. And what else is there but life?

Life.

What else is there but life?

Life.

And we are to put on our new
selves, because "just as you presented the
parts of your bodies as slaves to impurity
and to lawlessness for lawlessness, so now
present them as slaves to righteousness for

---

108 Sirach 21:11

sanctification."[109]

    Sanctification.

    Sanctification through temperance.

    Sanctification through temperance, because "sanctification's end is eternal life."[110]

    Eternal life.

    Eternal life, and what else is there, but eternal life?

    Eternal life.

        Eternal, life.

VIII.

    Life.

    Eternal life.

    And what else is there, but eternal life, through righteousness and justice.

    Righteousness is justice.

    Righteousness is justice, and "justice is rewarded."[111]

---

109 ROM 6:19

110 ROM 6:22

111 PS 58: 11-12

Rewarded.

Righteousness is justice, and justice is rewarded, because without reward there could be no justice; for what is justice if there is no right? And what is right if there is no reward? If there is no reward there is no need to be right. And so righteousness is justice, and justice is rewarded.

Rewarded.

Justice.

Justice.

Justice is goodness, and goodness is love.

Goodness is love.

Justice is goodness and goodness is love, and so justice is love.

Love.

Justice, more than any other virtue, is love.

Love.

Justice, more than any other virtue, is love, because love acts, and so justice acts.

Love, true love, acts; and justice, true justice, acts.

Acts.

Acts.

Justice is made true by action, and these actions are separated in two.

Two.

Two, "because justice gives God his due, and justice gives man his due."[112] God, and man. Two. Justice gives God his due, and justice gives man his due. Two.

Two.

And we are told by Jesus: two.

Two.

We are told by Jesus that there are two commandments: "Love God with all your heart, and all your soul, and all your mind, and love your neighbor as you love yourself."[113] God, and neighbor. God, and man. Two.

Two.

Love.

Two.

Two, because justice gives God his due, and his due is love; two, because justice gives man his due, and his due is love. And these are the two commandments, love God,

---

112 *Catechism of the Catholic Chutch*, 1807.
113 MT 22:37-39

love neighbor. And on these two commandments "depends the whole law."[114] The whole law. And what is law without justice.

Justice.

Justice is the righteous result of the law.

Justice is righteousness, and justice is goodness, and justice is love, and therefore justice is the whole law.

Justice is the whole law, and justice is a virtue.

Virtue.

Justice is a virtue, necessary for that most blessed, blessed virtue: love.

Love.

Love.

Love of God, love of neighbor. Love, an active love, a love that acts, an act of love in faith, because "faith without acts is dead."[115]

And these acts are love, based in love of the Father, and love of man.

Love.

---

114 MT 22:40

115 JAMES 2:17

There is love in justice, and justice in love.

Love.

And there is justice in faith, because "The just shall live by faith,"[116] and "the one who is just by faith will live."[117]

And so our justice should be large, as our love is to be large, because there is no other way. Our justice should be large as our love is to be large, because it is what He wants, it is what He expects, and we have been told that "unless your righteousness surpasses that of the Pharisees and the teachers of the law, you will certainly not enter the kingdom of heaven."[118]

Heaven.

Heaven.

Heaven through justice.

Justice.

Heaven through justice, because justice loves God and seeks to give God His due. Justice loves God and seeks to pray to God constantly, and to live for God

---

116 HEB 10:38
117 ROM 1:17
118 MT 5:20

307

devoutly, and to worship God perfectly, and to keep his word faithfully, and in this there is love.

Love.

In this there is love, and in giving God His due we cannot possibly refrain from giving man his due, because "If anyone says, "I love God," but hates his brother, he is a liar; for whoever does not love a brother whom he has seen cannot love God—whom he has not seen. This is the commandment we have from him: whoever loves God must also love his brother."[119]

Love.
Love of God, love of man.
Two.
Justice.
This is justice.
And justice is a virtue.
A virtue.
Justice is a virtue, that ever-so-crucial virtue, because justice is love.

Love.

---

119 1 JN 4:20-21

Justice is love.

Love.

Justice is love.

Love.

Love.

Justice.

Love.

Justice

Love.

Love.

Love.

Justice.

Love.

Love.

Justice, is love.

IX.

Love.

Love.

Love!

Love!

And now love, and so love.

Love.

Love.

Love.

What it is.

Love.

Fulfillment, depletion.

Fulfillment, by depletion.

Utter fulfillment.

Utter fulfillment.

Utter fulfillment, by our utter depletion; our depletion, with a purpose, our depletion, that does not leave us depleted, but exalted.

Exalted.

Exalted.

Love, true love, our depletion that does not leave us bereft of love, but as love itself, as love, as love itself, because that is love, true love, love itself, true love, love itself, is love.

Love.

Love.

Love, true love.

Love, love itself.

Love, what it is.

Love.

Love.

The object, the means.

Love.

Love, is the means, to the object, of

love.

Love, love itself.

Love, true love, love in the Truth, is

all.

All.

Love is all.

Love is all.

All.

Love is all.

The beginning, the ending.

Love.

Love is all.

The beginning, the ending.

It is obvious, to see; just look up,

just look up, it is obvious, to see.

Love is the beginning, and the

ending. The beginning, and the ending.

Because He is the beginning, and He is the

ending. The beginning, and the ending.

He is the beginning—the Alpha—and He is

the ending—the Omega—and He is love,

love. He is love, true love.

      "God is love."[120]

      God is love.

      God is love!

      God is love!

      "God is love," but we are not.

      Love is not us, but we can be love.

      Love is not us, but we can be love,
because He is in us, if we let Him be, and
He is love, love, and so can we be love, love.

      Love.

      Love is not us, but we can be love,
with Him, in us, if we let Him.

      If we let Him.

      If we let Him love, in us.

      If we let Him.

      Love.

      Love.

      Love, if we let Him love, in us,
because when He is in us, we cease to be for
us, but for Him, and when He is in us, we
will only be us, truly.

      Truly.

      When He is in us, we will only be

120 1 JN 4:16

us, truly, as He made us to be, for Him, and for love, He who is love, He who is love, He who is love, and so that we may become love, love.

Love.
Love.
"God is love."
"God is love."
"God is love."

And so can we be love, too. But not by ourselves. But only with Him. Because we are not ourselves without Him. We are not ourselves without Him. Without Him, we are nothing. Without Him, we are not love. Without Him, He who is. Without Him, He who will be. Without Him, we are nothing, we cease to be. We cease to be, without Him. And so with Him, we are. With Him, we are.

We are.

With Him, we are, and what else is there to be, but are?

What else, but are?

What else is there to be, but to be, to be, itself, to be, to exist, to exist for that

purpose for which we were created? If we
do not exist for that purpose for which we
were created, we will not be. We will not
be. We are, but we will not be.

We are, but we will not be.

Except through love.

Love.

Love, that enduring love.

Love, that love that is so real, that
love that is so hard, but only because we let
it be, we let it be, that love that is so hard,
but only because we let it be. And so we
should not just let it be. We should be. We
should be love.

Love.

We should be love, that enduring
love, because the only love that endures is
His love, love from Him and of Him, He
who endures. We do not endure, except
through Him, He who was and He who will
be; He who endures.

Endures.

Endures.

He who endures.

And so that is our goal, to be like

Him, to endure. We are to endure because enduring is life, true life, enduring is life itself. Life itself. Enduring is life itself, and there is no other life.

Life itself, to he who endures.

Through love.

And by love.

And with love.

Through Him.

With Him.

And in Him.

But only through Him.

Through His love.

He who loved us first, so that we may love at all.

He who loved us first, so that we are able to love at all.[121]

First.

He who loved us first, enabling us to love.

Love.

He who loved us first, enabling us to love.

Love.

---

121 1 JN 4:19

Love.

Love.

...

...

...because love!

Love!

Love!

Love!

What it is, love!

Love, what it is!

What it is, love!

Love!

Love!

Love!

What it is.

Love.

Love, love in our creation. Love, love in our creation, our very creation. Love, love in our creation, love in our free-will. Love in our free-will to love, or not love. To love, or not love. And love is a virtue.

A virtue.

Love is a virtue, and virtue is a choice.

The choice is ours. The choice is ours. The choice is ours.

Love, our choice.

Love, our choice, but only because He loved us first.

First.

He loved us first, and He loves us last, because of His love, love on the cross. Love, love by the cross. Love, love in the nails. Love, love in blood's drip, love in blood's most meaningful drip. Love, love in His blood, His most precious blood. Love, love in His blood, His most precious blood. Love, love in His blood.

Blood.

Love in His blood, His most precious blood.

Blood.

Love in His blood, His most precious blood.

Blood.

Love.

Love in His most precious blood, so that we know it will be okay.

Okay.

Okay.

Love in His most precious blood, so that we may know it will be okay.

Okay.

Okay.

And in this there is hope, bounding from faith, flowing from His blood, His most precious blood. Hope, bounding from faith, flowing from the love that is His most precious blood.

Love.

Love.

Love through His depletion, His utter depletion.

Love through His depletion, His utter depletion, by our hands, and because of us, yet for us, yet for us, yet for us, because this is His love, true love.

Love.

Love.

Love in depletion, utter depletion.

Love in depletion, selfless depletion.

Love.

Love.

Love exhaled, under God's son.

318

Love exhaled, under God's sun,
with Christ's last breath.

Love exhaled, with Christ's last
breath.

Breath, life.

Life.

Life!

Life!

Life!

Life exhaled, love exhaled.

Love exhaled with Christ's last
breath...

...our first breath!

Our first breath!

Love exhaled with Christ's last
breath, our first breath.

Our first breath, love.

Our first breath, love.

Love, our first breath, breathed, into
us, and not coming from us or by us. We,
us. Into us. Christ's last breath breathing
life, into us. Us. We. Life, true life,
breathed into us, through love, true love,
His love.

Love.

Love.

Love!

Love!

Love!

True life breathed into us through His love, true love.

And so are we to become life's breath, we are to become life's love.

Love.

Love.

We are to become life's breath, we are to become life's love. Under this most brilliant sun.

This sun.

This sun.

This most brilliant sun.

Sun.

Sun.

Sun, love.

Sun, love.

And but what is love?

Love.

And but what is love?

Love.

What is love?

Love.

Love, truly, is true love. Anything less than true love is less than true, and thus is not full, because true equals full, and anything less than full is partly empty, and partly empty is partly wanting and true love wants for nothing.

Nothing.

True love wants for nothing and we have been told, in the spirit of Truth, that we are to love, fully, with all our heart, all our mind, and all our soul.

This is our purpose in life. This is full love. This is true love. Truly.

Truly, this is love, true love. And truly, we cannot achieve this love on our own, or by ourselves, because this true love is His love, and is from Him, He who loved us first. We cannot achieve this love on our own, or by ourselves, because we are us, and we are not Him, and so we are not love, we can only become love, but only through Him, because to love the way He loves we must be less like ourselves and more like Him, and so His love—*His love*—must shine through us, by our depletion, our utter depletion, by our surrender, our utter surrender.

Surrender, our utter surrender, through our virtue.

Virtue.

Through our virtue.

Virtue.

Surrender, through our virtue, our utter surrender, through our virtue, which is not a hollowing out, but a true fulfillment.

Fulfillment.

Our surrender is not a hollowing out, but our life's fulfillment, our utter fulfillment—our realization of who we are meant to be.

Meant to be.

Our surrender is our realization of who we are meant to be; and why should we be anything other than what we were meant to be?

Be.

Why?

Why should we be anything other than what we were meant to be?

Be.

Why?

Why should we be anything other than what we were meant to be?

Be.

Be.

And so then, we are to be love, which is what we were meant to be.

We are to be love, which is what we

were meant to be.

    Love.

    Love.

    Love.

    But what is love?

    Love.

    What is love?

    Love is union

          ...with

            Him.

    Love is union

    ....

        with Him.

    Love is union, with Him, He who is, He who will be. Love is union, with Him, and what greater end can we possibly achieve? What greater end can we possibly achieve than to be, ourselves, eternal.

    Eternal.

    What greater end can we possibly achieve than to be eternal, in love, His love?

    Eternal, in love, His love, His perfect love. Love, His perfect love. There is no imperfection in perfection, and so there is no longing in love's perfection. There is no imperfection in perfection, and so in love, true love, eternal love, there is only true, unending, unsurpassed, blissful contentment.

Contentment, His placid, yet exuberant contentment.

Contentment.

Contentment.

Contentment, because this is all over.

This.

This is all over.

Contentment, because we are finally at home.

Contentment, in what is, and in what will be.

Contentment in He who is, and He who will be.

Contentment.

Contentment.

Love's deep sigh, contentment.

The end of all matters.

The end of all things.

The end of all matters.

The end of all things.

Love.

Love.

Love.

And finally, contentment.

Finally.

Finally.

Finally, contentment.

Contentment.

Contentment.

Contentment, love. Love from
contentment.

Love.

Love.

Love.

Love.

Love.

      ...and finally...

         ...finally...

           ...

           contentment.